Reprint Publishing

FOR PEOPLE WHO GO FOR ORIGINALS.

www.reprintpublishing.com

THE

COMPLETE

CONFECTIONER,

PASTRY-COOK. AND BAKER.

PLAIN AND PRACTICAL

DIRECTIONS FOR MAKING

CONFECTIONARY AND PASTRY,

AND FOR BAKING;

WITH UPWARDS OF FIVE HUNDRED RECEIPTS:

CONSISTING OF

DIRECTIONS FOR MAKING ALL SORTS OF PRESERVES,

SUGAR-BOILING, COMFITS, LOZENGES,

ORNAMENTAL CAKES,

ICES LIQUEURS, WATERS, GUM-PASTE ORNAMENTS
SYRUPS, JELLIES, MARMALADES, COMPOTES,

BREAD-BAKING,

ARTIFICIAL YEASTS, FANCY BISCUITS,

CAKES, ROLLS, MUFFINS, TARTS, PIES, &c. &c.

WITH ADDITIONS AND ALTERATIONS,
BY PARKINSON,
Practical Confectioner, Chestnut Street.

PHILADELPHIA:

J. B. LIPPINCOTT & CO.

1864.

PREFACE

TO THE AMERICAN EDITION.

———————

ALMOST every foreigner who visits this country remarks with astonishment the almost universal neg.ect
of that art upon which, more than any thing else, depends the health and comfort of a people ; and by many
scientific men have most of the prevalent diseases of
this country, especially the dyspepsia, been ascriben to
the hurried, crude and unwholesome manner in which
our food is prepared ; of latter years, more attention nas
been paid to cooking; but the handmaiden of that pa-
rent art, confectionary, is still neglected and unknown,
yet it is of little less importance than the graver branch
referred to. Confectionary is the poetry of epicurism
it throws over the heavy enjoyments of the table the
relief of a milder indulgence, and dispenses the delights
of a lighter and more harmless gratification of the ap-
petite. The dessert, properly prepared, contributes
equally to health and comfort; but " got up" as confectionary too often is, it is not only distasteful to a
correct palate, but is deleterious and often actually poisonous.

In introducing to the American public the modes by
which the table of hospitality may be enriched and

adorned, we have consulted every authority, French or English, within our reach; but the basis of our little work is to be found in Read's Confectioner, a late London publication.

Having for many years been connected with the oldest, most extensive and successful confectionary establishment in the country, we have been enabled to make from our own experience many important modifications and to introduce many additional receipts, particularly in relation to the various articles of luxury which the bounty of our soil and climate render almost exclusively American.

The volume has thus been increased in size, and we trust improved in value.

Trusting that our efforts to advance the popular knowledge of the art which has for many years engaged our attention, may meet with approbation, we present the result of our labours to a candid and indulgent public.

Chestnut Street,
    Philadelphia.

PREFACE

TO THE ENGLISH EDITION.

Much as there has been written in Cookery Books on the art of Confectionary, there are few, very few works on the subject now extant which are practically written, and these are difficult to be obtained, even at high prices; and, having been published some years since, they do not contain any of the modern improvements, or articles which have been introduced within these few years. The object of the present Treatise is to supply this deficiency, and to convey instruction in as plain and concise a manner as possible to the inexperienced, or young apprentices, that they may be enabled to learn their business more efficiently than many masters can or will instruct them in it.

The style and character of the present work will be found quite different from anything which has preceded it. In the part relating to Sugar-boiling I have endeavoured to show the causes of the effects which take place at the different stages, with the uses to which each of the processes is applied. The deficiency on Hard Confectionary which occurs in all other works will be found amply supplied in this. In the proportions for medicated lozenges I have preferred those which are ordered by the different Colleges of Surgeons in their pharmacopœias to those used by the trade, as being more likely to contain the true quantities of the different drugs which should compose them. It is from this source that they were originally derived, as at one time they formed no inconsiderable part of pharmacy; but they are now only made by confectioners.

The Section on Ices I have endeavoured to render as plain and intelligible as possible, and although I have given general as well as definite rules for the mixture of each sort, yet the last cannot at all times be implicitly followed, but must be modified or altered with respect to the flavouring matter so as to suit the taste of the employer or the parties for whom they are intended; this should always be most scrupulously attended to, if it is wished to give satisfaction as no fixed rules can be given which will admit of their being made to please all persons.

The business of confectionary is divided into several branches, some of them being quite distinct and separate from each other. The branch known as Hard Confectionary is literally the whole of the business, according to the strict meaning of the word, which is derived from the French words *confitures*—comfits, things crusted

1*

over with dry sugar; and *confiturier*—confectioner, a maker or seller
of comfits or other sweetmeats.   The other branches are the Ornamental and Soft Confectionary.   The latter relates to everything
connected with the oven, or all sorts of cakes and soft biscuits, and
more particularly to the preservation of fruits; the other, as the
name implies, to every description of ornaments necessary for the
decoration of the table.   Hard Confectionary still remains a distinct
branch or trade of itself; in fact, many persons' sole occupation is
the making of lozenges and comfits, termed pan-work.   Some also
combine with these the different articles connected with sugar-boiling
and preserving.   The latter are in general blended together, and
mostly practised by cooks and pastry-cooks; but the chief business
of a confectioner is alone connected with the ornamental department,
and everything necessary for the dessert.

I have thought it requisite to mention this specifically, so as to
prevent the occurrence of errors which parents and guardians of
families often fall into respecting the nature of the business, and also
with regard to the capacity of the child which they intend should be
brought up to it.   I have heard many say, "Never mind; he is a
stupid fool, and may do very well to make cakes."   If making *cakes*
were the sole object he would have to accomplish, *perhaps he might
do* very well; but even this requires more ingenuity than is generally
considered; and if the welfare of the child is studied, so as to enable
him to obtain his livelihood in a respectable manner, they must find
some means of enabling him to acquire a considerable deal more
knowledge than is general with a common-place education, to enable
him to compete with the talent at present in the labour-market.   The
person adapted for this business should be neat and cleanly in his
habits, of a lively and ingenious mind, have a quick conception of
design, a delicate taste, with a general knowledge of architecture,
mythology, and the fine arts; for they are as requisite in the construction of a Pièce Montée, or an allegorical subject to embellish
the table, as to an architect or sculptor in the construction of an expensive building or monument.   I do not mean to infer that his in-
formation must be so extensive, or that he will be required to make
the tour of Italy, Rome, and Greece, to study the original masters;
but let him take Nature for his guide; and if he possess the rudi-
ments or principles of the art of design, he cannot fail, with a little
attention and perseverance, to become an adept in the higher or ornamental branches of his business.

CONTENTS.

THE CONFECTIONER.

viii

CONTENTS.

THE PASTRY-COOK.

THE BAKER.

THE CONFECTIONER.

~~~~~~~~~~~~~~~

SECTION I.—CONFECTIONARY.

As sugar is the basis or ground-work of the confectioner's art, it is essentially necessary that the practitioner should carefully study and observe the difference in its qualities, the changes which it undergoes or effects when combined with other articles in the process of manufacture, and also the different forms which it assumes by itself at various stages.   Without this knowledge, a man will never become a thorough and efficient workman, and it can only be acquired by practice and experience.

The first process which it undergoes in the hands of the confectioner, is that of clarification.   It is conducted on the same principle as the refining of sugar, although not carried out in every particular.

Clarification of Raw Sugar.—For every six pounds of sugar required to be clarified, take one quart of water, the white of an egg, and about half a teacupful of bullock's blood.   Less than a pint will be sufficient for 112 pounds; but if a very fine, transparent, and colourless syrup is required, use either charcoal, finely powdered, or ivory black, instead of the blood.   Put the white of the egg in the water and whisk it to a froth, then add either of the other articles mentioned, and the sugar, place the pan containing the ingredients on the stove-fire, and stir them well with a spatula, until the sugar is dissolved, and is nearly boiling.   When the ebullition commences, throw in a little cold water to check it; this causes the coarser parts to separate more freely, by which means the whole of the impurities attach themselves to the clarifying matter used; continue this for about five minutes, using about one pint of water to every six pounds of sugar, or more, until you consider the whole of the dross is discharged, and there remains a fine clear syrup.   Then place it by the side of the stove, and carefully remove with a skimmer the scum which has formed on the top: it may also be taken off as it rises, but I find the best method is to let it remain a short time after it is clarified before it is removed, otherwise, if you take it off as it rises, part of the syrup is also taken with it.   When either charcoal or black is used, it must be passed through a filtering-bag made of thick flannel, in the shape of a cone, having a hoop fastened round the top to keep it extended, and to which strings are sewn that it may be tied or suspended in any convenient manner: what runs out at first will be

13

quite black; return this again into the bag, and continue doing so until it runs fine and clear.

If a little lime, about a spoonful, or any other alkali is added to the sugar with the water, &c., it will neutralize the acid which all raw sugars contain, and they will be found to stand much better after they have been manufactured, by not taking the damp so soon. This is not generally done by the trade, but it will be found beneficial if practised.

To clarify Loaf Sugar.—This is clarified by mixing the whites of eggs with water, without any other assistance, for having been previously refined, it does not require those auxiliaries again to separate the coarser parts, unless it is of an inferior quality, or an extra fine syrup, as for bon-bons and other fancy articles, is required. When it is necessary to have a very fine sparkling grain, in that case break your lump into small pieces and put it in a preserving-pan, with a sufficient quantity of water to dissolve it, in which has been mixed the white of an egg and powdered charcoal,* as for raw sugar, following those instructions already given. After the sugar has been drained from the bag, pass some water through to take off any which may be left in the charcoal, which you use for dissolving more sugar.

The scum should always be reserved, when charcoal or black is not used, to mix with the articles of an inferior quality.

The best refined loaf sugar should be white, dry, fine, of a brilliant sparkling appearance when broken, and as close in texture as possible. The best sort of brown has a bright, sparkling, and gravelly look. East India sugars appear finer, but do not contain so much saccharine matter, yet they are much used for manufacturing the best sort of common sweetmeats, when clarified, instead of loaf sugar.

Degrees of boiling Sugar.—This is the principal point to which the confectioner has to direct his attention; for if he is not expert in this particular, all his other labour and knowledge will be useless: it is

---

*Charcoal varies in its qualities, according to the wood from which it is prepared. That made from porous woods, such as the willow, alder, &c., is the best for clarifying liquids; animal charcoal, or bone black, is also equally good, on account of its light and porous nature; that made from hard woods is only fit for fuel, as it does not possess the clarifying and decolouring properties like that made from the more soft and porous woods. When newly prepared, or if it has been kept free from air, it has the property of absorbing all putrid gases; " it is also capable of destroying the smell and taste of a variety of animal and vegetable substances, especially of mucilages, oils, and of matter in which extractive abounds; and some articles are said to be even deprived of their characteristic odour, by remaining in contact with it, as valerian, galbanum, balsam of Peru, and musk. The use of charring the interior of water-casks, and of wrapping charcoal in cloths that have acquired a bad smell, depend upon this property. None of the fluid menstrua with which we are acquainted have any action whatever, as solvents, upon carbon."— *Paris's Pharmacologia.*

the foundation on which he must build to acquire success in his undertakings.

There are seven essential points or degrees in boiling sugar; some authors give thirteen, but many of these are useless, and serve only to show a critical precision in the art, without its being required in practice; however, for exactness, we will admit of nine, viz.—1. Small thread. 2. Large thread. 3. Little pearl. 4. Large pearl. 5. The blow. 6. The feather. 7. Ball. 8. Crack. 9. Caramel. This last degree derives its name from "a Count Albufage Caramel, of Nismes, who discovered this method of boiling sugar."—*Gunter's Confectioner.*

In describing the process, I shall proceed in a different manner to other writers on the subject, by classing it under different heads, according to the uses to which it is applied.

SYRUP.

Under this head are comprised the degrees from the small thread to the large pearl; for at these points the sugar is kept in a divided state, and remains a fluid of an oily consistency. A bottle which holds three ounces of water will contain four ounces of syrup. The method of ascertaining those degrees, according to the usages of the trade, is as follows:—

Small Thread.—Having placed the clarified syrup on the fire, let it boil a little, then dip the top of your finger in the boiling syrup, and on taking it out apply it to the top of your thumb, when, if it has attained the degree, on separating them a small ring will be drawn out a little distance, about as fine as a hair, which will break and resolve itself into a drop on the thumb and finger.

Large Thread.—Continue the boiling a little longer, repeat the same operation as before, and a larger string will be drawn.

Little Pearl.—To ascertain this degree, separate the finger from the thumb as before, and a large string may be drawn, which will extend to nearly the distance the fingers may be opened.

Large Pearl.—The finger may now be separated from the thumb to the greatest extent before the thread will break.

CRYSTALLIZATION.

This takes the degrees of the blow and feather. The particles of the sugar being now brought together within the sphere of their activity, the attraction of cohesion commences, whereby they attach themselves together and form quadrilateral pyramids with oblong and rectangular bases. This is generally, but improperly, termed candy, thereby confounding it with the degrees at which it grains, also termed candy. This certainly seems "confusion worse confounded;" but if things are called by their proper names, many of those seeming difficulties and technicalities may be avoided which tend only to confuse and embarrass the young practitioner, without gaining any desired end or purpose. If it were generally classed into the degrees of crystallization, the true meaning and use would at once be explained and understood by the greatest novice.

The nature and principle of this operation are these. First, as in the case of syrup (the first four degrees), *when the water has absorbed as much sugar as it is capable of containing in a cold state,* by continuing the boiling, a further portion of the solvent (water) is evaporated, and sugar remains in excess, which, when exposed to a less degree of heat, separates itself, and forms crystals on the surface and sides of the vessel in which it is contained, and also on anything placed or suspended in it. But if it is exposed too suddenly to the cold, or disturbed in its action by being shaken, or if the boiling has been continued too long, the crystals will form irregularly by the particles being brought in too close contact, and run too hastily together, forming a mass or lump.

To obtain this part in perfection, the boiling should be gradual, and continued no longer than till a few drops let fall on a cold surface show a crystalline appearance, or after being removed from the fire a *thin* skin will form on the surface. It should then be taken from the fire and placed in *a less hot but not cold* place, and covered or put into a stove or hot closet to prevent the access of cold air. A few drops of spirits of wine, added when the sugar has attained the proper degree, will conduce to a more perfect crystalline form, scarcely attainable by any other means, as it has a great affinity with the water, thereby causing the sugar to separate itself more freely. It must be used with caution, as too much will cause it to grain.

To ascertain the Degree of the Blow.—Continue the boiling of the sugar, dip a skimmer in it and shake it over the pan, then blow through the holes, and if small bubbles or air-bladders are seen on the other side, it has acquired this degree.

The Feather.—Dip the skimmer again into the sugar, and blow through the holes as before, and the bubbles will appear larger and stronger. Or if you give the skimmer a sudden jerk, so as to throw the sugar from you, when it has acquired the degree, it will appear hanging from the skimmer in fine long strings.

CANDY.

Sugar, after it has passed the degree of the feather, is of itself naturally inclined to grain, that is to candy, and will form a powder if agitated or stirred : for as the boiling is continued, so is the water evaporated until there is nothing left to hold it in solution : therefore that body being destroyed by heat, which first changed its original form to those we have already enumerated, as this no longer exists with it, it naturally returns to the same state as it was before the solvent was added, which is that of minute crystals or grains, being held together by the attraction of cohesion, unless, as before stated, they are separated by stirring, &c.

The sugar being evaporated by boiling from the last degree, leaves a thin crust of crystals round the sides of the pan, which shows it has attained the candy height; and this crust must be carefully removed, as it forms, with a damp cloth or sponge, or the whole mass will candy if suffered to remain. To prevent this is the chief desideratum, all further proceedings for which specific rules will be given in their proper places.

The remaining degrees can be ascertained after the following manner:—

The Ball.—Provide a jug of clean cold water, and a piece of round stick. First dip in the water, then in the sugar, and again in the water;* take off the sugar which has adhered to it, and endeavour to roll it into a ball between the finger and thumb in the water: when this can be done, it has attained the desired degree. If it forms a large hard ball which will bite hard and adhere to the teeth when eaten, it is then termed the large ball, *et contra.*

The Crack.—Follow the directions given for the ball. Slip the sugar off from the stick, still holding it in the water, then press it between the finger and thumb; if it breaks short and crisp, with a slight noise, it is at the crack.

Caramel.—To obtain this degree it requires care and attention, and also to be frequently tried, as it passes speedily from the crack to the caramel. Try it as before directed, and let the water be quite cold, or you will be deceived. If on taking it off the stick it snaps like glass, with a loud noise, it has attained the proper degree; it will also, when it arrives at this point, assume a beautiful yellow colour; after this it will speedily burn, taking all the hues from a brown to a black; therefore, to prevent this, dip the bottom of the pan into a pail of cold water as soon as it comes to caramel, as the heat which is contained in the pan and sugar is sufficient to advance it one degree; also be careful that the flame of the fire does not ascend round the sides of the pan, which will burn it.

In boiling sugar, keep the top of the pan partially covered from the time it commences boiling until it has attained the ball or crack: the steam which rises, being again thrown on the sides, prevents the formation of the crust or crystals.

To prevent its graining, add a little of any sort of acid when it is at the crack—a table-spoonful of common vinegar, four or five drops of lemon-juice, or two or three drops of pyroligneous acid: any of these will have the desired effect; this is termed greasing it: but remember that too much acid will also grain it, neither can it be boiled to caramel if there is too much. A little butter added when it first commences boiling will keep it from rising over the pan, and also prevent its graining. About as much cream of tartar as may be laid on a sixpence, and added to seven pounds of sugar with the water, or equal quantities of cream of tartar and alum in powder, added when

* This should be performed as speedily as possible.

14

it boils, will also keep it from candying. If sugar is poured on a slab that is too hot it is very apt to grain; this is frequently the case after several casts have been worked off in rotation; therefore, when you find it inclined to turn, remove it to a cooler spot, if possible, and not handle it any more than is necessary.

Sugar that has been often boiled or warmed is soon acted upon by the atmosphere, whereby it becomes clammy and soon runs, as it is weakened by the action of the fire. Acid causes the same effect.

If it has passed the degree you intended to boil it at, add a littl water, and give it another boil.

SECTION II.—SYRUPS.

These are either the juices of fruits, or a decoction or infusion of the leaves, flowers, or roots of vegetables, impregnated with a sufficient quantity of sugar for their preservation and retaining them in a liquid state.

A great portion of this class comes more under the notice of the apothecary than the confectioner; but it may now be considered, with lozenges, as a branch of pharmacy in the hands of the latter, the most agreeable of which are now manufactured by him to supply the place of fresh fruits, &c., when out of season, for the making of cooling drinks, ices, &c., for balls and routs.

General Rules and Observations.—Two things are essentially necessary to be observed, which are:—the proper methods of making decoctions and infusions. These require some knowledge of the nature and properties of vegetable matter.

The virtues of most plants are extracted by infusion, and this is generally the case with aromatic plants, and those whose properties depend on an essential oil; for, in boiling, the whole of the aroma of the plant is dispersed, and the syrup loses that delicate flavour for which it is prized.

Aromatic herbs, and the leaves of plants in general, yield their virtues most perfectly when moderately dried. Cold water extracts from these in a few hours, the lighter, more fragrant and agreeable parts, and then begins to take up the more ungrateful and grosser. By pouring the same liquor on fresh parcels of the herb, it becomes stronger, richer, thicker, and balsamic.

Those only should be decocted whose principles consist of mucilage, gum, or resin, and require boiling to extract them.

The compact resinous woods, roots and barks, yield their virtues most freely while fresh. Dry, they yield little to cold or moderately warm water, and require it to be boiling. By this process the grosser, more fixed saline and mucilaginous parts are dissolved, the resinous melted out, and the volatile dissipated.

Infusions. — " These are watery solutions of vegetable matter obtained by maceration, either in hot or cold water, with the assistance of ebullition. In selecting and conducting the operation. the following general rules should be observed :—

" 1st. Infusion should always be preferred before decoction, where the virtues of the vegetable substance reside in volatile oil, or in principles which are easily soluble ; whereas, if they depend upon resino-mucilaginous particles, decoction is an indispensible operation.

" 2nd. The temperature employed must be varied according to the circumstances of each case, and infusion made with cold is in general more grateful but less active than one made with heat.

" 3rd. The duration of the process must likewise be regulated by the nature of the substances ; for the infusion will differ according to the time in which the water has been digested on the materials ; thus the aroma of the plant is first taken up, then in succession the colouring, astringent, and gummy parts.

Decoctions.—" These are solutions of the active principles of vegetables, obtained by boiling them in water.

" 1st. Those principles only should be decocted whose virtues reside in principles which are soluble in water.

" 2nd. If the active principle be volatile, decoction must be an injurious process; and if it consists of extractive matter, long boiling, by favouring its oxidizement, will render it insipid, insoluble, and inert.

" 3rd. The substances to be decocted should be previously bruised or sliced, so as to expose an extended surface to the action of the water.

" 4th. The substances should be completely covered with water, and the vessel slightly closed, in order to prevent as much as possible the access of air ; the boiling should be continued without interruption, and gently.

" 5th. In compound decoctions, it is sometimes convenient not to put in all the ingredients from the beginning, but in succession, according to their hardness, and the difficulty with which their virtues are extracted; and if any aromatic or other substances containing volatile principles, or oxidizable matter, enter into the composition, the boiling decoction should be simply poured upon them, and covered up until cold.

" 6th. The relative proportions of different vegetable substances to the water must be regulated by their nature. The following general rule may be admitted. Of roots, barks, or dried woods, from two drachms to six to every pint of water: of herbs, or flowers, half that quantity will suffice.

" 7th. The decoction ought to be filtered through linen while hot, as important portions of the dissolved matter are frequently deposited on cooling ; care must also be taken that the filter is not too fine, for it frequently happens that the virtues of a decoction depend upon the presence of particles in a minutely divided state." — *Paris's Pharmacologia.*

All acid syrups ought to have their full quantity of sugar, so as to bring them to a consistence without boiling, because the very actnt of much heat destroys their acidity, and makes them liable to candy, and this more particularly holds good where the infusion or juice, &c. has any fragrancy in flavour, because the volatile oil is dissipated by boiling. The same observation is also applicable to those infusions of flowers which give out their colour, and which is necessary to be retained, such as violets, pinks, &c., as boiling injures them.

Those syrups which are made from decoctions, and do not take a sufficient quantity of sugar to bring them to a due consistence without boiling, require to be clarified so as to render them transparent; but this is often an injury, as the whites of eggs take off some of their chief properties with the scum; therefore, the decoction should first be rendered clear by settling or filtering, and the sugar should be clarified and boiled to the height of the feather or ball before the decoction is added, when it must be reduced to the proper degree.

The best and most general method of making syrups is to add a sufficient quantity of the finest loaf-sugar, in powder, with the juice or infusion, &c., stirring it well until a small portion settles at the bottom, then place the pan in a larger one containing water; this is termed the bain-marie; put it on the fire, and the heat of the water as it boils will dissolve the sugar; when this has been thoroughly effected, take it off and let it cool; if more sugar is added than the quantity above named, it will separate in crystals, and not leave sufficient remaining in the syrup for its preservation. (See observations on Sugar-boiling). When cold, put it into small bottles, fill them, cork closely, and keep in a dry cool place. Be particularly careful that no tinned articles are used in the making of syrups from the juice of red fruits, as it will act on the tin and change the colour to a dead blue.

Raspberry Syrup.—One pint of juice, two pounds of sugar. Choose the fruit either red or white, mash it in a pan, and put it in a warm place for two or three days, or until the fermentation has commenced. All mucilaginous fruits require this, or else it would jelly after it is bottled. Filter the juice through a flannel bag, add the sugar in powder, place in the bain-marie, and stir it until dissolved; take it off, let it get cold, take off the scum, and bottle it.

[*Pine-apple Syrup.*—Take one and a half pints of syrup boiled to the ball, add to this, one pint of the juice of the best Havanna pine-apples; let it then come to a boil, remove the scum, and bottle when cool.]

Raspberry Vinegar Syrup.—One pint of juice, two pints of apple vinegar, four pounds and a half of sugar. Prepare the juice as before, adding the vinegar with it, using white vinegar with white raspberries; strain the juice and boil to the pearl.

Three pounds of raspberries, two pints of vinegar, three pounds of sugar. Put the raspberries into the vinegar without mashing them, cover the pan close, and let it remain in a cellar for seven or eight days: then filter the infusion, add the sugar in powder, and finish in the bain-marie. This is superior to the first, as the beautiful aroma of the fruit is lost in the boiling, as may be well known by its scenting the place where it is done, or even the whole house; the fruit may also be afterwards used with more for raspberry cakes.

[*Strawberry Syrup.*—Make as pine-apple; taking care to strain carefully at least twice, through a fine flannel bag, so as to remove entirely all sediment, and the small seed of the fruit.]

Currant Syrup.—One pint of juice, two pounds of sugar. Mix together three pounds of currants, half white and half red, one pound of raspberries, and one pound of cherries, without the stones; mash the fruit and let it stand in a warm place for three or four days, keeping it covered with a coarse cloth, or piece of paper with holes pricked in it to keep out any dust or dirt. Filter the juice, add the sugar in powder, finish in the bain-marie, and skim it. When cold, put it into bottles, fill them, and cork well.

Morello Cherry Syrup.—Take the stones out of the cherries, mash them, and press out the juice in an earthen pan; let it stand in a cool place for two days, then filter; add two pounds of sugar to one pint of juice, finish in the bain-marie, or stir it well on the fire, and give it one or two boils.

Mulberry Syrup.—One pint of juice, one pound twelve ounces of sugar. Press out the juice and finish as cherry syrup.

Gooseberry Syrup.—One pint of juice, one pound twelve ounces of sugar. To twelve pounds of ripe gooseberries add two pounds of cherries without stones, squeeze out the juice, and finish as others.

Lemon Syrup.—One pint and a quarter of juice, two pounds of sugar. Let the juice stand in a cool place to settle. When a thin skin is formed on the top, pour it off and filter, add the sugar, and finish in the bain-marie. If the flavour of the peel is preferred with it, grate off the yellow rind of the lemons and mix it with the juice to infuse, or rub it off on part of the sugar and add it with the remainder when you finish it.

Orange Syrup.—As lemon syrup.

Orange-Flower Syrup.—Picked orange flowers one pound, sugar three pounds. Take one half of the sugar and make a syrup, which boil to the large pearl, put the flowers in a basin or jar, and pour the syrup on them boiling hot, cover the jar or basin quite close and let them infuse in it for five or six hours, then drain off the syrup, boil the remaining portion of sugar, and pour over them as before; when cold, strain and bottle.

Sirop de Capillaire.—*Syrup of Maidenhair.*—There are several sorts of Maidenhair, but the best is that of Canada, which has a pleasant smell joined to its pectoral qualities. The true Maidenhair—*Capillus Veneris*—is a native of Italy and of the southern parts of France. It has an agreeable but very weak smell. Common or English Maidenhair—*Trichomanes*—is usually substituted for the true, and occasionally for the Canadian. Its leaves consist of small round divisions, growing as it were in pairs. It grows on rocks, old

wells, and shady banks, and should be gathered in September
Black Maidenhair—*Adianthum Nigrum*—has smooth and shining
leaves, the middle rib being black, and the seeds are all spread on the
back of the leaf. It grows on shady banks, and on the roots of trees.
White Maidenhair—Wall Rue—Tent Wort—*Ruta Murana Salvia
Vitæ.*—The leaves of this are shaped something like rue, and covered
all over the back with a small seed-like dust. Golden Maidenhair—
Muscus Capillaris—grows in moist places, and the pedicle arises
from the top of the stalk. I have given these particulars, because I
find they are often substituted one for the other by persons who are
not aware that there is any difference. Although all of them have
nearly the same qualities, only two have a volatile oil, but they are
all mucilaginous.

Canada capillaire two ounces, sugar two pounds. Chop the
capillaire into small bits, and make as orange-flower syrup. By this
method the oil is not allowed to escape, which being exceedingly
odoriferous and volatile, is soon dissipated if boiled ; or make a cold
infusion (See Infusions) of the plant by putting one quart of water to
four ounces of capillaire, add four pounds of sugar, and finish in the
bain-marie, adding one ounce of orange-flower water.* [This is a
fashionable and delicate syrup, but is rarely obtained genuine.]

Simple syrup, flavoured with orange-flower water, is usually substituted for it.

Syrup of Liquorice.—Liquorice-root two ounces, white maidenhair
one ounce, hyssop half an ounce, boiling water three pints ; slice the
root and cut the herbs small, infuse in the water for twenty-four
hours, strain and add sufficient sugar, or part sugar and honey, to
make a syrup; boil to the large pearl. An excellent pectoral.

Syrup of Violets.—One pound of violet flowers, one quart of water,
four pounds of sugar. Put the flowers cleared from their stalks and
calx, into a glazed earthen pan ; pour on the water boiling hot, and
stop the pan quite close; let it remain in a warm place for a day,
then strain off the infusion through a thin cloth; add the sugar, and
place in the bain-marie : stir it well and heat it until you can scarcely
bear your finger in it; then take it off, and when cold, bottle. A
laxative. This syrup is often adulterated by being made with the
flowers of hearts-ease, or columbine scented with orrice-root, and
coloured.

Syrup of Pinks.—Clove pinks, one pound eight ounces, water
two pints and a half, sugar, three pounds. Let the flowers be fresh
gathered, cut off the white points of the petals and weigh them.
Finish as syrup of violets. This syrup may be made with a cold in-

* The pectoral quality of this syrup—for it is often sold for such pur
poses in shops—would be much improved if made with the addition of
liquorice-root, as ordered by the Pharmacopœias—" Five ounces of capillaire, two ounces of liquorice-root, six pints of water ; white sugar a
sufficient quantity ; two ounces of orange-flower water "

fusion of the flowers, first pounding them with a little water in a marble mortar. Finish as before. If the flowers of the clove pink cannot be obtained, use other pinks, adding a few cloves to infuse with them, so as to give the flavour.

Syrup of Roses.—The dried leaves of Provence roses eight ounces double rose leaves six ounces, water one quart, sugar four pounds. Pour the water on the leaves when nearly boiling, into a glazed earthen vessel, cover it quite close, and let it remain in a warm place for a day; then strain and finish as violets. The leaves of the damask rose are purgative.

Syrup of Wormwood.—There are three sorts of wormwood most generally known,—the common, sea, and Roman. The first may be distinguished by its broad leaves which are divided into roundish segments, of a dull green colour above, and whitish underneath; its taste is an intense and disagreeable bitter. The sea wormwood has smaller leaves and hoary both above and underneath; it grows in salt marshes, and about the sea coasts; the smell and taste are not so strong and disagreeable as the common. The Roman differs from the others by the plant being smaller in all its parts; the leaves are divided into fine filaments and hoary all over, the stalk being either entirely or in part of a purple colour. Its smell is pleasant, and the bitterness not disagreeable: it is cultivated in gardens. The sea wormwood is generally substituted for it.

The tops of Roman wormwood two ounces, water one pint, sugar two pounds. Make an infusion of the leaves in warm water, strain, add the sugar to the infusion, and boil to the pearl. If the common wormwood only can be obtained, put the tops into three times the above quantity of water, and boil it over a strong fire until reduced to a pint. This will deprive it of part of its bitterness and disagreeable smell.

Syrup of Marshmallows—Sirop de Guimauve.—Fresh mallow roots eight ounces, water one quart, sugar three pounds. Cleanse the roots, and slice them; make a decoction (See Decoctions). boiling it a quarter of an hour, so as to obtain the mucilage of the root; strain, and finish as wormwood. One ounce of liquorice-root and one ounce of white maidenhair, with a few stoned raisins, may be added.

[*Syrup of Sarsaparilla.*—Half a pound of bruised sarsaparilla root, two ounces of ground orange peel, one ounce liquorice-root, sassafras bark bruised, two ounces, one gallon of water; boil to half a gallon, strain; to each pint of liquor add one pound of sugar; put on the fire till it boils, and take off the scum which arises.]

Syrup of Coltsfoot.—Fresh Coltsfoot flowers one pound eight ounces, water one quart, sugar three pounds. Pick the flowers about February, and make an infusion of them with hot water; strain, and finish as wormwood syrup. Two or three handfuls of the leaves may be pounded and infused instead of the flowers.

Syrup of Ginger.—Ginger two ounces, water one pint, sugar two pounds.

Slice the root if fresh, or bruise it if dried; pour the water on it boiling, and let it macerate in a warm place for a day, then strain, and boil to the pearl.

[*Another.*—A better flavoured and a richer ginger syrup is made in the following manner.—Take any quantity of scraped, white, Jamaica ginger and infuse for several days in good spirits of wine; decant the clear liquor when sufficiently saturated with the ginger, and add to the hot sugar, previously boiled to the ball or feather, a sufficient quantity of the liquor to impart to the syrup the agreeable aroma of the ginger root.

The spirit will be rapidly driven off when it is poured into the boiling syrup, and a bland and beautiful syrup will be the result; let it cool, and bottle immediately.]

Syrup of Almonds — Sirop de Orgeat. — One pound of sweet almonds, four ounces of bitter ones, one pint and a half of water, sugar three pounds, orange-flower water two ounces.

Blanch the almonds, and as they are blanched throw them into cold water; when they are finished, take them out and pound them in a marble mortar, sprinkling them with a little orange-flower water to prevent their oiling, or use water with the juice of a lemon; add sufficient in the pounding to reduce them to a paste, and when quite fine add half a pint more water; mix, and strain through a tamis cloth twisted tight by two persons: receive the milk which comes from the almonds into a basin; what is left in the cloth must be pounded again with some of the water, and strained. Continue this until the whole of the milk is obtained, and the water, is consumed; then clarify, and boil the sugar to the crack; add the milk of almonds, and reduce it to the pearl; then strain it again, add the orange-flower water, and stir it well until nearly cold; when cold, bottle; shake the bottles well for several succeeding days, if you see it at all inclined to separate, which will prevent it.

Sirop de Pistache is made in the same manner, colouring it green with a little spinach.

Syrup of Coffee.—Fresh roasted Mocha coffee two pounds, water one quart, sugar three pounds eight ounces. Grind the coffee in mill, and make a cold infusion with the water in a close vessel; let it stand for a day, then filter it through blotting paper; add the sugar, and finish in the bain-marie.

Syrup of Rum Punch.—Jamaica rum one quart, the juice of twelve or fourteen lemons, sugar four pounds. Rub off the yellow rind of half of the lemons on a piece of the sugar, and scrape it off with a knife into a basin as it imbibes the oil; clarify and boil the remaining portion to the crack; strain the juice into the rum, and add to it the sugar with that on which the peels were rubbed; mix together, and give it one boil. The yellow rind of the peels may be cut off very thin, and infused in the spirit for some days before the syrup is made

Brandy and Wine Syrups may be made in the same manner.

SECTION III.—CRYSTALLIZED SUGAR, AND ARTICLES CRYSTAL-
LIZED, COMMONLY CALLED CANDIES.

Crystallized or Candied Sugar.—Provide a round mould, smaller at
the bottom than the top, of any size you may think proper, made
either of tin or copper, with holes pierced round the sides about three
inches asunder, so as to fasten strings across in regular rows from the
top to the bottom, leaving sufficient room for the sugar to crystallize
on each string without touching, or it will form a complete mass;
paste paper round the outside to prevent the syrup from running
through the holes. Have the mould prepared, and let it be clean and
dry; take sufficient clarified syrup to fill the mould, and boil it to the
degree of crystallization or the feather, and add a little spirit of wine;
remove it from the fire, and let it rest until a thin skin is formed on
the surface, which you must carefully remove with a skimmer; then
pour it into the mould, and place it in the hot closet, where you let it
remain *undisturbed* for eight or nine days, at 90 degrees of heat, or
half that time at 100; then make a hole, and drain off the super-
fluous sugar into a pan placed below to receive it; let it drain quite
dry, which will take about twelve hours; then wash off the paper
from the mould with warm water, place it near the fire, and keep
turning it to warm it equally all round; then turn it up and strike
the mould rather hard upon the table, when the sugar will relieve
itself and come out: put it on a stand or sieve in the closet, raise the
heat to 120 degrees, and let it remain until perfectly dry. Particular
attention should be paid to the heat of the closet, which must be kept
regular and constant, and this can easily be accomplished at a small
expense with many of the patent stoves which are now in general
use, and also without causing any dust. A Fahrenheit's or Reaumur's
thermometer should be so placed that the heat may at all times be
ascertained.

This may be coloured with prepared cochineal, or other liquid
colour, or by grinding any particular colour with the spirits of wine,
and adding it to the syrup before it comes to the feather.

Fruits to Crystallize.—Have a square or round tin box, smaller at
the bottom than the top, with wire gratings made to fit at convenient
distances, and having a hole with a tube or pipe to admit a cork, and
drain off the syrup. Take any of the preserved fruits wet (which
see), drain from them the syrup, and dip them in lukewarm water to
take off any syrup which may adhere to them; dry them in the
closet; when dried, place them in layers on the gratings, side by
side, so as not to touch each other; continue in this manner with any
sort of fruit until the box is full; then fix the whole with a weight,
to keep it steady. Boil a sufficiency of clarified sugar to fill the box
to the degree of crystallization or the blow, add a little spirit of wine,
and remove it from the fire. When a thin skin has formed on the top,
remove it carefully with a skimmer, and pour the sugar into the

mould ; place it in the closet at 90 degrees of heat, and let it remain for twelve hours, then drain off the syrup into a pan from the tube at bottom, and let it remain in the closet until quite dry ; then turn them out by striking the box hard upon the table, separate them carefully, and put them in boxes with paper between each layer. When different fruits, paste, knots, &c., are mixed together indiscriminately, it is termed mille-fruit candy. Any sort of fruit or gum pastes, when thoroughly dried, may be crystallized in the same manner. When the syrup is drained off, if you find the size of the crystals is not large enough, another lot of syrup may be prepared and poured over it ; let it remain in the closet for seven or eight hours, then drain and finish as before.

If small pieces of stick are pushed down at each corner, or in any other vacancy, when you fill the mould, one of these may be withdrawn at any time you may wish to ascertain the size of the crystals, which will save the trouble of giving a second charge of sugar.

Crystallized Chocolate.—Prepare some sugar, as in the preceding articles, and pour it into the box. When a thin crust is formed on the top, make a hole on one side, and push the articles previously shaped with chocolate, as for drops, gently under with your finger ; put them in the stove to crystallize, as other articles. After the syrup is drained off, and the articles dried, they must remain until quite cold before being turned out, as the chocolate continues soft for some time.

Liqueur Rings, Drops, and other Devices.—These are all made after the same manner. A square box is necessary, which you fill with very dry starch powder. Sugar, powdered very fine and dried, will answer the same purpose. The depth of the box should be suited to the articles intended to be made. Shake the box, or pass a knife repeatedly through the powder, that it may be solid ; smooth the surface with a straight piece of wood ; have a thin piece of flat board, on which is fastened a number of little devices, about an inch asunder, and to suit the width of the box; these may be made either of lead, plaster, or wood, in the form of rings, diamonds, stars, bottles, scissors, harps, shoes, or any other form your fancy may suggest; make the impressions in the powder in regular rows, until the box is full ; then prepare some sugar as for the preceding articles, boiling it to the blow, and flavouring it with any sort of spirit or liqueur, such as brandy, rum, noyau, Maraschino, cinnamon, rosolis, &c., colouring the syrup accordingly. It should be prepared in a pan with a lip to it. When a thin skin has formed on the top, place a cork in the lip of the pan, but not to close it, allowing a space for the sugar to run out, the cork being merely to keep back the skin ; then fill the impressions you made in the powder and place them in the stove at 90 degrees ; let them remain a day, then take them out, and their surfaces will be found quite hard and solid ; brush the powder from them with a light brush, when they may either be painted, crystallized, or piped. Many of these bon-bons are beautifully piped and coloured to represent dogs, horses, costumes, and theatrical characters; the fur on the robes is imitated with white or coloured sugar in coarse grains, and lace-work is done by means of a pin.

Liqueur drops are made with the impression of half a ball to any required size, or other forms. If the flat parts of two are moistened, put together, and dried in the stove, they will form drops perfectly round.

To form a Chain with Liqueur Rings.—Have some moulds to form the impressions in powder, as in the preceding, in the shape of the links of a chain; fill them with syrup at the blow, as before, and put them in the stove for a day; when they are hard and fit to be taken out, place them on their ends in the powder; have another mould of a link in two halves, and with this form the impression between each of the others so as to make it complete; then fill them, and finish as before.

SECTION IV.—CANDY—BONBON—CONSERVE.

THE articles that come under this head are made by the sugar being brought to the ball, when it is grained by rubbing it against the sides of the pan. From this all fancy articles are made, such as fruit, eggs, cups, vases, &c.

Ginger Candy.—Take clarified syrup and boil it to the ball; flavour it either with the essence of ginger or the root in powder; then with a spoon or spatula rub some of it against the side of the pan until you perceive it turn white; pour it into small square tins with edges, or paper cases, which have been oiled or buttered, and put it in a warm place, or on a hot stone, that it may become dappled. The syrup should be coloured yellow, while boiling, with a little saffron.

Peppermint, Lemon and Rose Candy are made after the same manner, colouring the lemon with saffron, and the rose with cochineal.

Coltsfoot or Horehound Candy.—Make a strong infusion of the herbs, (See Infusions under the head of Syrups,) and use it for dissolving the sugar, instead of taking syrup; raw sugar is mostly used for those candies. Boil it to the ball, grain it and finish as ginger candy.

Artificial Fruit, Eggs, &c.—Prepare moulds with plaster of Paris from the natural objects you wish to represent; make them in two, three, or more pieces, so as to relieve freely, and have a hole at one end into which the sugar may be poured; let them be made so as each part may be fitted together exactly; and for this purpose make two or three round or square indentions on the edge of one part, so that the corresponding piece when cast, will form the counterpart, which may at all times be fitted with precision. Let the object you would take the cast from be placed in a frame made either of wood or of stiff paper, embed a part of it in fine sand, soft pipe-clay, or modelling wax, leaving as much of the mould exposed as you wish to form at one time, and oil it with sweet oil; mix some of the prepared plaster with water, to the consistency of thick cream, and pour over it; when this is set, proceed with the other portions in the same manner until it is complete. Let them dry and harden for use.

Take a sufficient quantity of syrup, (clarified with charcoal or animal black) to fill the mould, and boil it to the small ball; rub some of it against the side to grain it; when it turns white, pour it into the moulds: take them out when set, and put them into the stove at a moderate heat to dry. The moulds must be soaked for an hour or two in cold water previously to their being used, which will be found better than oiling them, as it keeps the sugar delicately white, which oil does not. Colour your articles according to nature with liquid colours (see Colours) and camel's-hair pencils, or the usual pigments sold in boxes may be used. If a gloss is required, the colours should be mixed with a strong solution of gum Arabic or isinglass, to the desired tint. Eggs and fruit may be made as light and apparently as perfect as nature, by having moulds to open in two, without any orifice for filling them. Fill one half with the grained sugar, immediately close the mould, and turn it round briskly that it may be covered all over equally. To accomplish this, it is necessary to have an assistant that it may be done as speedily as possible.

Burnt Almonds.—Take some fine Valencia or Jordan almonds, and sift all the dust from them; put a pint of clarified syrup into the pan for each pound of almonds, and place it with the almonds on the fire; boil to the ball, then take it off and stir the mixture well with a spatula that the sugar may grain and become almost a powder, whilst each almond has a coating. Put them into a coarse wire or cane sieve, and sift all the loose sugar from them, and also separate those which stick together. When cold, boil some more clarified syrup to the feather, put in the almonds, give them two or three boils in it, take them from the fire, and stir them with the spatula as before, until the sugar grains; sift and separate them, and keep them in glasses or boxes. A third coat may be given them in the same manner as the second, if they are required large.

Burnt Almonds—Red.—The same as the last, using prepared cochineal to colour the syrup whilst it is boiling.

Filberts and Pistachios.—These are done the same as burnt almonds, but they are usually denominated prawlings, the nuts being only put into the sugar for two or three minutes before it is taken from the fire, and stirred.

Common Burnt Almonds.—These are made with raw sugar and skimmings, if you have any. Put some water with the sugar to dissolve it; when it is near boiling, add the almonds, and let them boil in it until it comes to the small ball; or when the almonds crack, take them from the fire, and stir them with a spatula until the sugar grains and becomes nearly a powder; put them into a sieve, and separate the lumps.

Orange Prawlings.—Take four or five Havanna oranges, and cut off the peel in quarters, or small lengths; take off all the pith or white part of the peel, leaving only the yellow rinds, and cut in small pieces, about an inch long, and the size of pins. Have about a pint of clarified sugar boiling on the fire; when it comes to the blow, put in the pieces of peel, and let them boil until the sugar attains the small ball; take them off, and stir them with the spatula until the sugar grains and hangs about them; sift off the loose sugar; when cold, separate and keep them in a dry place.

Lemon Prawlings.—As orange.

SECTION V.—CRACK AND CARAMEL.

THESE comprehend all articles in sugar-boiling which eat short and crisp. They are used for all sorts of ornamental sugar-work. The rules and observations already laid down under this head must be particularly noted, especially those for greasing the sugar so as to prevent its graining.

Barley Sugar.—Boil some clarified loaf sugar to the crack or caramel degree, using a little acid to prevent its graining: pour it out on a marble slab, which has been previously oiled or buttered. Four pieces of iron, or small square bars, are usually employed to form a sort of bay to prevent the sugar running off the stone, which is necessary in large casts. When the edges get set a little, remove the bars, and turn them over into the centre. This is occasionally flavoured with lemons. When it is required, pour a few drops of the essential oil of lemons in the centre, before the edges are folded over, then cut it into narrow strips with a large pair of scissors or sheep-shears. When nearly cold, twist them, put them into glasses or tin boxes, and keep them closed to prevent the access of air. It is seldom boiled higher than the crack, and saffron is used to make it the colour of caramel.

This derives the name of barley sugar from its being originally made with a decoction of barley, as a demulcent in coughs, for which it is now most generally used.

Barley Sugar Drops.—Boil some sugar as for the preceding. Spread some finely powdered and sifted loaf sugar on a table or tea-tray, with a piece of stick, round at the end similar to the half of a ball; make several holes, into which you run the sugar from a lipped pan, or it may be dropped on an oiled marble slab with a funnel, letting only one drop fall at a time; or from the lip pan, separating each drop with a small knife, or a straight piece of small wire; take them off the stone with a knife, mix them with powdered loaf sugar, sift them from it, and keep in glasses or tin boxes.

Barley Sugar Tablets or Kisses.—Spread some sugar, as for the last have a piece of wood about an inch and a half thick, with the surface divided into small squares, each being about an inch, and half an inch in depth; with this form the impressions in the sugar, and fill them with sugar boiled as for drops, flavouring it with essence of lemon; or instead of this it may be poured out in a sheet on an oiled marble slab, as for barley sugar, and when nearly cold divide it into pieces with a tin frame, having small square divisions, when the whole sheet may be divided at once by pressing hard on it so as to cut it nearly through. When cold, separate them and mix them with powdered sugar, take them out and fold them separately in fancy or coloured papers, with a motto on each. They are also occasionally made into balls thus:—First cast the sugar in a sheet on an oiled marble slab; when the edges are set, fold them in the middle, then oil a small square tin with edges to it, put the sugar in this, and place it under the fire-place of the stove so as to keep warm; cut off a piece and roll it into a pipe, then cut it into small pieces with a pair of shears, and let your assistant roll it into small balls under his hand on a sand-stone; marble is too smooth for this purpose. Many lads who are used to it can turn eight or ten under each hand at one time. When they are finished, put them into powdered sugar, wrap them in fancy papers, fringed at the ends, put a motto in each, and fasten them with small bands of gold paper. Sometimes a cracker is folded up in each, which is made with two narrow strips of stiff paper, a small piece of sand or glass paper is pasted on the end of each, and these are placed over each other with a little fulminating powder between, a piece of thin paper is bound round it, and pasted to keep them together; when these are pulled asunder, the two rough surfaces meeting cause the powder to explode, and out flies the ball of sugar with the motto. This innocent amusement often causes much mirth in a company.

Acid Drops and Sticks.—Boil clarified sugar to the crack, and pour it on an oiled marble stone: pound some tartaric or citric acid to a fine powder, and strew over it about a half or three quarters of an ounce of the former, according to its quality, and less of the latter, to seven pounds of sugar; turn the edges over into the middle, and mix the acid by folding it over, or by working it in a similar manner as dough is moulded, but do not pull it; put it in a tin rubbed over with oil or butter, and place it under the stove to keep warm; then cut off a small piece at a time, and roll it into a round pipe; cut them off in small pieces the size of drops, with shears, and le your assistant roll them round under his hand, and flatten them. Mix them with powdered sugar, sift them from it, and keep them in boxes or glasses.

When flavoured with lemon, they are called lemon-acid drops,—with otto of roses, rose-acid drops. The sticks are made in the same manner as the drops, without being cut into small pieces.

To extract the Acid from Candied Drops, &c.—All the articles which have acid mixed with them are extremely liable to grain, when they are useless for any purpose whatever, except to sell for broken pieces, as they cannot be boiled again unless the acid is extracted. The method of doing this is at present not generally known in the trade, and it is kept by many that are in possession of it as a great secret. A sovereign is often paid for this recipe alone. However great the secret may be considered, it is only returning to the first principle in the manufacture of sugar. When the juice is expressed from the canes, it contains a considerable quantity of oxalic acid, which must be destroyed before it will granulate into sugar: for this purpose lime is employed, which has the desired effect; so will it also in this case, but chalk or whitening is most generally used. First dissolve your acid sugar in water; when this is thoroughly accomplished, mix in a sufficient quantity of either of these alkalies in powder to cause a strong effervescence; after it has subsided, pass it through a flannel bag, according to the directions for clarifying sugar. The filtered syrup will be fit to use for any purpose, and may be boiled again to the crack or caramel degrees as well as if no acid had ever been mixed with it. Let the pan it is dissolved in be capable of containing as much again as there is in it, or the effervescence will flow over.

Raspberry Candy.—This may either be made from raw or refined sugar. Boil it to the crack, and colour it with cochineal; pour it on a stone rubbed over with a little oil or butter, cut off a small piece, and keep it warm to stripe or case the other part, when finished; to the remainder add a little tartaric acid (not so much as for drops), and some raspberry-paste, sufficient to flavour it. The residue of raspberries used for making vinegar, and preserved with an equal quantity of sugar, or even less, as for raspberry cakes, does very well for this purpose. Fold the edges over into the centre, and attach it to a hook fixed against the wall: pull it towards you, throwing it on the hook each time after having pulled it out; continue doing this until it gets rather white and shining, then make it into a compact long roll, and either stripe it with the piece you cut off, or roll it out in a sheet with a rolling-pin, and wrap it round it so as to form a sort of case; then pull it into long narrow sticks, and cut them the required length.

Clove, Ginger, or Peppermint Candy.—These are all made in the same way as raspberry, using the essential oil of each for flavour. For clove, the mixture, whilst boiling, is coloured with cochineal; ginger with saffron; but the peppermint must be kept perfectly white, except the stripes, which is done by cutting off as many pieces from the bulk as you have colours, which should be in powder; put a sufficiency in each piece to give the desired tint, and keep them warm. When the remaining portion of the sugar is pulled, lay them over the surface in narrow stripes, double the roll together, and the face each way will be alike. Pull them out into long sticks, and twist them; make them round by rolling them under the hand, or they may be cut into small pieces with a pair of shears or scissors.

Brandy Balls, &c.—These are made from loaf sugar, boiled to the crack, and coloured either with cochineal or saffron, and finished in the same way as acidulated drops, without being flattened.

Nogat.—Two pounds of sweet almonds, one pound of sugar, one pound of water. Blanch the almonds, and cut them in slices, dry them at the mouth of a cool oven, and if slightly browned the better; powder the sugar, and put it into a stewpan, with the water; place it on the fire to melt, stirring it with a spatula until it becomes a fine brown, then mix in the almonds, and let them be well covered with the sugar; pour it out on an oiled marble stone. It may be made into a thick or thin sheet, and cut with a knife into small pieces, such as dice, diamonds, &c. The surface may be strewed with currants, fillets of pistachios, or coarse sugar, and cut into different forms with tin cutters. It may also be formed into baskets, vases, &c. Oil the interior of a mould, and spread the nogat over it, whilst warm, as thin and even as possible. To save the fingers from being burnt, it may be spread with a lemon. Detach it from the mould when warm, and let it remain until cold that it may retain its shape perfectly, then fasten the different parts together with caramel sugar. For baskets, a handle of spun sugar may be placed over it, or ornamented with it according to fancy. These may be filled with whipped or other creams when required to be served.

Almond Rock.—This is a similar production to nogat, and is made with raw sugar, which is boiled to the crack. Pour it on an oiled stone, and fill it with sweet almonds, either blanched or not; the almonds are mixed with the sugar by working them into it with the hands, in a similar manner as you would mix anything into a piece of dough. If they were stirred into the sugar in the pan it would grain, which is the reason why it is melted for nogat. Form the rock into a ball or roll, and make it into a sheet, about two inches thick, by rolling it with a rolling-pin. The top may be divided into diamonds or squares by means of a long knife or piece of iron: when it is nearly cold cut it into long narrow pieces with a strong knife and hammer.

Almond Hardbake.—Oil a square or round tin with low edges; split some almonds in half, put them in rows over the bottom, with the split side downward, until the surface is covered; boil some raw sugar to the crack, and pour it over them so as to cover the whole with a thin sheet of sugar. Cocoa nut, cut in thin slices, currant, and other similar candies, are made as the hardbake, except that the sugar is grained before it is poured over.

ON SUGAR-SPINNING.

To attain proficiency in this part, it requires much practice, and also a good taste for design, and to be expert in the boiling of sugar, taking particular care to avoid its graining. Baskets, temples, vases, fountains, &c., are made by these means. It may almost be termed the climax of the art. The moulds for this purpose may be made either of copper or tin, so as to deliver well. Let them be slightly rubbed all over, on the part you intend to spin the sugar, with butter or oil.

Boil clarified syrup to the degree of caramel, taking care to keep the sides of the pad free from sugar. The moment it is at the crack, add a little acid to grease it (see Sugar Boiling). When it has attained the required degree, dip the bottom of the pan into cold water, take it out, and let it cool a little; then take a common table-spoon, dip it in the sugar, holding the mould in your left hand, and from the spoon run the sugar over the mould, either inside or out, with the threads which flow from it, which may be either fine or coarse, according to the state of the sugar; if they are required very coarse, pass the hand over them two or three times; for when it is hot it flows in finer strings than it will when cooler; form it on the mould into a sort of trellis-work; loosen it from the mould carefully, and let it remain until quite cold before it is taken off, that it may retain its shape. When the sugar gets too cold to flow from the spoon, place it by the side of the stove or fire to melt. Young beginners had better draw their designs for handles of baskets, &c., on a stone with a pencil before it is oiled, and then spin the sugar over them.

To make a Silver Web.—Boil clarified syrup to the crack, using the same precautions as before observed, giving it a few boils after the acid is added; dip the bottom of the pan in water and let the sugar cool a little; then take the handle of a spoon, or two forks tied together, dip it into the sugar, and form it either on the inside or outside of a mould, with very fine strings, by passing the hand quickly backwards and forwards, taking care that it does not fall in drops, which would spoil the appearance of the work. With this may be represented the hair of a helmet, the water of a fountain, &c. Take a fork, or an iron skewer, and hold it in your left hand as high as you can, dip the spoon in the sugar, and with the right hand throw it over the skewer, when it will hang from it in very fine threads of considerable length.

To make a Gold Web.—Boil syrup to caramel height, colouring it with saffron, and form it as directed for the last. It can be folded up to form bands or rings, &c. Fasten it to the other decorations with caramel.

If any of the strings or threads of sugar should pass over those parts where they are not required, so as to spoil the other decorations in the making of baskets or other ornaments, it may be removed with a hot knife without breaking or injuring the piece.

Chantilly Baskets.—Prepare some ratafias, let them be rather small, and as near of a size as possible; boil some sugar to the caramel degree, rub over the inside of a mould slightly with oil, dip the edge of the ratafias in sugar, and stick them together, the face of the ratafias being towards the mould, except the last two rows on the top, which should be reversed, remembering always to place their faces to meet the eye when the sugar is cold; take it out, and join the bottom and top together with the same sugar; make a handle of spun sugar, and place over it. Some sugar may be spun over the inside of the basket, to strengthen it, as directed for webs. Line the inside with pieces of Savoy or sponge cakes, and fill it with custard or whipped cream, or the slices of cake may be spread with raspberry jam. Half fill it with boiled custard, then put in a few Savoy or almond cakes, soaked in wine, and cover the top with whipped cream; or it may be filled with fancy pastry, or meringues. All sorts of fancy cakes may be made into baskets or ratafias.

Grape, Orange, or Cherry Baskets.—These are made similar to the last; the oranges are carefully peeled and divided into small pieces, taking off the pith. Insert a small piece of stick or whisk in the end of each, dip them in caramel, and form them on the inside of an oiled mould. Cherries and grapes may be used either fresh, or preserved wet, and dried. Dip them in caramel, and form them as oranges. Each of these, or any other fruit, after being dipped in caramel, may be laid on an oiled marble slab separately, and served on plates in a pyramid, with fancy papers, flowers, &c. The baskets are finished as Chantilly with spun sugar.

Almond Baskets.—Blanch some fine Jordan almonds, and cut them into thin slices, and colour them in a small copper pan over the fire with prepared liquid colour (see Colours). Put them into the pan, and pour in colour sufficient to give the desired tint; rub them about in the pan with your hand until they are quite dry: form them as for a Chantilly basket, or else form them on an oiled marble slab, and spin sugar over them on each side. Afterwards arrange them in a mould, or build them to any design, first having a pattern cut out in paper, and form them on the stone from it.

Spanish Candy.—Oil a quart of clarified syrup to the crack. Have some icing previously prepared as for cakes, or mix some fine powdered loaf sugar with the white of an egg to a thick consistency as for icing; take the sugar from the fire, and as soon as the boiling has gone down stir in a spoonful of this or the icing, which must be done very quickly, without stopping. Let it rise once and fall; the second time it rises, pour it out in a mould or paper case, and cover it with the pan to prevent its falling. Some persons pour it out the first time it rises, and immediately cover it as before. It may be made good both ways. If it is required coloured, add the colouring to the syrup whilst it is boiling, or with the icing, adding more sugar to give it the same stiffness as before.

Vases or Baskets, &c., in Spanish Candy.—Prepare some plaster moulds, as for grained sugar; soak them in water before you use them; prepare some sugar as for the last, and fill the moulds. When finished they may be ornamented with gum-paste, piping, or gold-paper borders. Fill them with flowers, meringues, fancy pastry, caramel, fruits, &c. They may also be made in copper or tin moulds, by first oiling them before they are filled.

SECTION VI.—CHOCOLATE.

Cacao Nuts.—The cocoa or cacao nut, of which chocolate is made, is the seed of the fruit of a tree common in South America and the West Indies. The seeds of the nuts, which are nearly of the shape of an almond, are found to the number of from thirty to forty in a pod. The pods are oval, resembling a cucumber in shape. The different sorts are distinguished by name, according to the places which produce them, thus,—the cacao of Cayenne, Caraccas, Berbice, and the islands of St. Magdalen and Domingo. These all differ in the size of their almonds or seed, quality and taste. The most esteemed is the large Caraccas, the almond of which, though somewhat flat, resembles the shape of a large bean. The next are those of St. Magdalen and Berbice. The seeds of these are less flat than those of the Caraccas kind, and the skin is covered with a fine ash-coloured dust. The others are very crude and oily, and only fit to make the butter of cacao. The kernels, when fresh, are bitter, and are deprived of this by being buried in the ground for thirty or forty days. Good nuts should have a thin brittle skin, of a dark black colour; and the kernel, when the skin is taken off, should appear full and shining, of a dusky colour, with a reddish shade. Choose the freshest, not worm-eaten, or mouldy on the inside, which it is subject to be.

Equal parts of the cacao of Caraccas, St. Magdalen, and Berbice, mixed together, make a chocolate of first-rate quality; and these proportions give to it that rich and oily taste which it ought to have. That made from the cacao of Caraccas only is too dry, and that from the islands too fat and crude.

Roasting.—Take a sufficient quantity of nuts to cover the bottom of an iron pot two or three inches deep, place them on the fire to roast, stirring them constantly with the spatula that the heat may be imparted to them equally. A coffee-roasting machine would answer for this purpose admirably, taking care not to torrefy them too much, as the oil of the nut suffers thereby, and it becomes a dark brown or black, grows bitter, and spoils the colour of the chocolate. Musty or mouldy nuts must be roasted more than the others, so as to deprive them of their bad taste and smell. It is only necessary to heat them until the skin will separate from the kernel on being pressed between the fingers. Remove them from the fire, and separate the skins. If you have a large quantity, this may be accomplished by putting them in a sieve which has the holes rather large, but not so much as to allow the nuts to pass through; then squeeze or press them in your hands, and the skins will pass through the meshes of the sieve; or, after being separated from the nuts, they may be got rid of by winnowing or fanning them in a similar manner to corn. When they are separated, put them again in the fire, as before directed, stirring them constantly until warmed through, without browning. You may know when they are heated enough by the outside appearing shiny again winnow, to separate any burnt skin which may have escaped the first time.

The Making of Chocolate.—An iron pestle and mortar is requisite for this purpose, also a stone of the closest grain and texture which can be procured, and a rolling-pin made of the same material, or of iron. The stone must be fixed in such a manner that it may be heated from below with a pot of burning charcoal, or something similar.

Warm the mortar and pestle by placing them on a stove, or by means of charcoal, until they are so hot that you can scarcely bear your hand against them. Wipe the mortar out clean, and put any convenient quantity of your prepared nuts in it, which you pound until they are reduced to an oily paste into which the pestle will sink by its own weight. If it is required sweet, add about one-half, or two-thirds of its weight of loaf sugar in powder; again pound it so as to mix it well together, then put it in a pan, and place it in the stove to keep warm. Take a portion of it and roll or grind it well on the slab with the roller (both being previously heated like the mortar) until it is reduced to a smooth impalpable paste, which will melt in the mouth like butter. When this is accomplished, put it in another pan, and keep it warm until the whole is similarly disposed of; then place it again on the stone, which must not be quite so warm as previously, work it over again, and divide it into pieces of two, four, eight, or sixteen ounces each, which you put in moulds. Give it a shake, and the chocolate will become flat. When cold it will easily turn out.

The moulds for chocolate may either be made of tin or copper, and of different devices, such as men, animals, fish, culinary or other utensils, &c.; also some square ones for half-pound cakes, having divisions on the bottom which are relievoed. These cause the hollow impressions on the cakes.

The Bayonne or Spanish chocolate is in general the most esteemed. The reason of its superior quality is attributed by some to the hardness of the Pyrenean stone which they employ in making it, which does not absorb the oil from the nuts. They do not use any pestle and mortar, but levigate their nuts on the stone, which is fixed on a slope; and in the second pounding or rolling the paste is pressed closely on the stone, so as to extract the oil, which runs into a pan containing the quantity of sugar intended to be used, and is placed underneath to receive it; the oil of the cacao and sugar are then well mixed together with a spatula, again mixed with the paste on the stone, and finished.

Vanilla Chocolate.—Ten pounds of prepared nuts, ten pounds of sugar, vanilla two ounces and a half, cinnamon one ounce, one drachm of mace, and two drachms of cloves, or the vanilla may be used solely.

Prepare your nuts according to the directions already given. Cut the vanilla in small bits, pound it fine with part of the sugar, and mix it with the paste; boil about one-half of the sugar to the blow before you mix it to the chocolate, otherwise it will eat hard. Proceed as before, and either put it in small moulds or divide it in tablets, which you wrap in tinfoil. This is in general termed eatable chocolate.

Cinnamon, Mace or Clove Chocolate.—These are made in the same manner as the last, using about an ounce and a half or two ounces of either sort of spice, in powder, to that quantity, or add a sufficiency of either of these essential oils to flavour.

Stomachic Chocolate.—Four ounces of chocolate prepared without sugar, vanilla one ounce, cinnamon in powder one ounce, ambergris forty-eight grains, sugar three ounces; warm your paste by pounding in the heated mortar, or on the stone, add your aromatics in powder to the sugar, and mix it well with the paste; keep it close in tin boxes. About a dozen grains of this is to be put into the chocolate pot when it is made, which gives it an agreeable and delightful flavour, and renders it highly stomachic. It may also be used for flavouring the chocolate tablets.

Chocolate Harlequin Pistachios. — Warm some sweet chocolate by pounding it in a hot mortar; when it is reduced to a malleable paste, take a little of it and wrap round a blanched pistachio nut, roll it in the hand to form it as neat as you can, throw it in some nonpareils of various colours; let it be covered all over. Dispose of the whole in the same manner; fold them in coloured or fancy papers, with mottoes, the ends should be cut like fringe. Almonds may be done the same way, using vanilla chocolate, if preferred.

Chocolate Drops, with Nonpareils. Have some warm chocolate, as for pistachios; some add a little butter or oil to it to make it work more free; make it into balls about the size of a small marble, by rolling a little in the hand, or else put some of the paste on a flat piece of wood, on which you form, and take them off with a knife. Place them on sheets of white paper about an inch apart. When the sheet is covered, take it by the corners and lift it up and down, letting it touch the table each time, which will flatten them. Cover the surface entirely with white nonpareils, and shake off the surplus ones. When the drops are cold they can be taken off the paper easily. The bottom of the drops should be about as broad as a sixpence. Some of them may be left quite plain.

Good chocolate should be of a clear red brown. As the colour is paler or darker, so is the article the more or less good. The surface should be smooth and shining. If this gloss comes off by touching, it indicates an inferior quality, and is probably adulterated. When broken, it ought to be compact and close, and not appear crumbly. It should melt gently in the mouth when eaten, leaving no roughness or astringency, but rather a cooling sensation on the tongue. The latter is a certain sign of its being genuine.

SECTION VII.—LOZENGES.

THESE are composed of loaf sugar in fine powder, and other substances, either liquid or in powder, which are mixed together and made into a paste with dissolved gum, rolled out into thin sheets, and formed with tin cutters into little cakes, either oval, square, or round, and dried.

One ounce of gum tragacanth, and one pint of water. Let it soak in a warm place twenty-four hours; put it in a coarse towel or cloth, and let two persons continue twisting it until the whole of the gum is squeezed through the interstices of the cloth. One ounce of this dissolved gum is sufficient for four or five pounds of sugar; one ounce of dissolved gum Arabic to twelve ounces of sugar.

Either of these gums may be used separately, or in the proportion of one ounce of gum dragon to three ounces of Arabic mixed together. These are generally used for medicated lozenges; but gum Arabic alone is considered to make the best peppermint.

Peppermint Lozenges, No. 1. — Take double-refined loaf sugar, pound and sift it through a lawn sieve; make a bay with the sugar on a marble slab, into which pour some dissolved gum, and mix it into a paste as you would dough, flavouring the mass with oil of peppermint. One ounce of this is sufficient for forty pounds of lozenges. Some persons prefer mixing their gum and sugar together at first in a mortar; but as it is indifferent which way is pursued, that may be followed which is most convenient. Roll out the paste on a marble slab until it is about the eighth of an inch in thickness, using starch powder to dust it with, to prevent its sticking to the slab and pin. Before cutting them out, strew or dust over the surface with powder mixed with lawned sugar, and rub it over with the heel of your hand, which gives it a smooth face. This operation is termed "facing up." Brush this off, and again dust the surface with starch powder, cut them out, and place in wooden trays. Put them in the hot closet to dry. *Note.*—All lozenges are finished in the same manner.

Peppermint Lozenges, No. 2.—These are made as No. 1, adding a little starch-powder or prepared plaster as for gum paste to the paste, instead of using all sugar.

Peppermint Lozenges, Nos. 3 *and* 4.—Proceed in the same manner as for No. 2, using for each, more starch powder in proportion. Use smaller cutters, and let the paste be rolled thicker.

Transparent Mint Lozenges, No. 5. — These are made from loaf sugar in coarse powder, the finest having been taken out by sifting it through a lawn sieve. Mix it into a paste with dissolved gum Arabic and a little lemon juice. Flavour with oil of peppermint. Finish as for No. 1.

Superfine Transparent Mint Lozenges.—The sugar for these must be in coarser grains. Pass the sugar through a coarse hair sieve. Separate the finest by sifting it through a moderately fine hair sieve. Mix and flavour as the others.

Note.—The coarser the grains of sugar, the more transparent the lozenges. The finer particles of sugar being mixed with it, destroy their transparency. The solution of gum should be thicker in proportion as the sugar is coarse.

Rose Lozenges.—Make your paste as No. 1, using the essential oil or otto of roses to flavour them; or the gum may be dissolved in rose water, and a little essential oil may be added to give additional flavour, if required. Colour the paste with carmine or rose pink.

Cinnamon Lozenges. — Gum tragacanth, dissolved, two ounces, lawned sugar eight pounds, cinnamon in powder one ounce, essential oil ten drops.

Mix into a paste, and colour with bole ammoniac. A stomachic.

Clove Lozenges. — Sugar eight pounds, cloves three ounces, gum tragacanth two ounces.

Each lozenge should contain two grains of cloves. A restorative and stomachic.

Lavender Lozenges.—Make as rose lozenges, using the oil of lavender instead of rose.

Ginger Lozenges.—Eight pounds of sugar and eight ounces of the best ground ginger. Mix into a paste with dissolved gum. Essence may be used instead of the powder, colouring it with saffron. A stimulant and stomachic.

Nutmeg Lozenges.—Sugar eight pounds, oil of nutmegs one ounce, dissolved gum sufficient to mix into a paste. A stimulant and stomachic.

Rhubarb Lozenges. — Sugar four pounds, best Turkey rhubarb, in powder, ten ounces.

Sulphur Lozenges. — Four pounds of sugar, eight ounces of sublimed sulphur, gum sufficient to make a paste. For asthma and the piles.

Tolu Lozenges.—Sugar four pounds, balsam of tolu three drachms, or the tincture of the balsam one fluid ounce, cream of tartar six ounces, or tartaric acid one drachm, dissolved gum sufficient to make a paste. These may also be flavoured by adding a quarter of an ounce of vanilla, and sixty drops of the essence of amber. The articles must be reduced to a fine powder with the sugar. A pectoral and balsamic.

Ipecacuanha Lozenges.—Sugar four pounds, ipecacuanha one ounce, apothecaries' weight, dissolved gum sufficient to make a paste. Make 960 lozenges, each containing half a grain of ipecacuanha. An expectorant and stomachic, used in coughs.

Saffron Lozenges.—Saffron dried and powdered, four ounces, suga four pounds, dissolved gum sufficient. An anodyne, pectoral, cm menagogue.

Yellow Pectoral Lozenges.—Sugar one pound, Florence orris-root powder twelve drachms, liquorice-root, six drachms, almonds one ounce, saffron in powder four scruples, dissolved gum sufficient to make a paste. Make a decoction of the liquorice to moisten the gum with.

Lozenges for the Heartburn.—Prepared chalk four ounces, crab's eyes prepared two ounces, bole ammoniac one ounce, nutmeg one scruple, or cinnamon half an ounce. Make into a paste with dissolved gum Arabic.

Steel Lozenges.—Pure iron filings or rust of iron one pound, cinnamon in powder, four ounces, fine sugar seven pounds, dissolved gum a sufficient quantity to make a paste. A stomachic and tonic.

Magnesia Lozenges.—Calcined magnesia eight ounces, sugar four ounces, ginger in powder two scruples, dissolved gum Arabic sufficient to form a paste.

Magnesia two ounces, sugar eight ounces, sufficient gum Arabic to make a paste, dissolved in orange-flower water.

Nitre Lozenges.—Sugar four pounds, sal-nitre one pound, dissolved gum tragacanth, sufficient to make a paste. A diuretic internally; held in the mouth it removes incipient sore throats.

Marshmallow Lozenges.—Marshmallow roots in powder one pound, or slice the root and make a strong decoction, in which you dissolve the gum, fine sugar four pounds. Mix into a paste. If six drops of laudanum be added, with two ounces of liquorice, the pectoral quality of these lozenges will be improved. Good for obstinate coughs.

Vanilla Lozenges.—Sugar four pounds, vanilla in powder, six ounces, or sufficient to give a strong flavour. Make into a paste with dissolved gum.

Catechu Lozenges.—Sugar four pounds, catechu twelve ounces. Make into a paste with dissolved gum.

Catechu à l'Ambergris.—To the paste for catechu lozenges add sixteen grains of ambergris.

Catechu with Musk.—The same as for catechu, adding sixteen grains of musk.

Catechu with Orange-flowers.—As before, adding twelve drops of essence of neroli.

Catechu with Violets.—As before, adding Florence orris-root in powder, three drachms. These are all used to fasten the teeth, and disguise an offensive breath.

Ching's Yellow Worm Lozenges.—Fine sugar twenty-eight pounds, calomel washed in spirits of wine one pound, saffron four drachms, dissolved gum tragacanth sufficient to make a paste. Make a decoction of the saffron in one pint of water, strain, and mix with it. Each lozenge should contain one grain of mercury.

Ching's Brown Worm Lozenges.—Calomel washed in spirits of wine (termed *white panacea of mercury*), seven ounces, resin of jalap three pounds eight ounces, fine sugar nine pounds, dissolved gum sufficient quantity to make a paste. Each lozenge should contain half a grain of mercury.

Panacea, one ounce, resin of jalap two ounces, sugar two pounds. Dissolve a sufficient quantity of gum in rose-water to make a paste. Make 2520 lozenges, weighing eight grains each, and containing a quarter of a grain of calomel and half a grain of jalap.

These lozenges should be kept very dry after they are finished, as the damp, acting on the sugar and mercury, generates an acid in them.

Note.—In mixing *these*, as well as all other medicated lozenges, the different powders should be well mixed with the sugar, in order that each lozenge may have its due portion. If this is not attended to, the perfect distribution of the component parts cannot be depended on, and one lozenge may contain double or treble the quantity of medicated matter it ought to have, whilst others contain comparatively none; therefore those that have the greatest portion may often prove injurious by acting contrary to what was intended.

Bath Pipe.—Eight pounds of sugar, twelve ounces of liquorice. Warm the liquorice and cut it in thin slices, dissolve it in one quart of boiling water, stir it well to assist the solution; let it settle, when dissolved, to allow any impurities or bits of copper which are often found in it to fall down; pour it off free from the sediment; dissolve the gum in the clear part, and mix into a paste as for lozenges. Roll out a piece with your hand in a round form; finish rolling it with a long flat piece of wood, until it is about the size of the largest end of the stem of a tobacco-pipe. Dry them in the stove as lozenges. These may be also flavoured with anise-seed by adding a few drops of the oil, or with catechu or violets by adding the powders of orris-root or catechu.

Peppermint or other Pipes.—Any of the pastes for lozenges may be formed into pipes by rolling it out as directed for Bath pipes. They are occasionally striped with blue green, and yellow, by making strips with liquid colour on the paste and twisting before you roll it out with the board.

Brilliants.—Take either of the pastes for peppermint lozenges from No. 1 to 4, and cut it into small fancy devices, such as hearts, diamonds, spades, triangles, squares, &c.

Refined Liquorice.—Four pounds of the best Spanish juice, and two pounds of gum Arabic. Dissolve the gum in warm water, as for Bath pipe. Strain and dissolve the gum in the solution of liquorice. Place it over a gentle fire, in a broad pan, and let it boil gradually, stirring it continually (or it will burn) until it is reduced to a paste. Roll it into pipes or cylinders of convenient lengths, and polish by putting them in a box and rolling them together, or by rubbing them with the hand, or a cloth. This is often adulterated by using glue instead of gum, and by dipping the pipes in a thin solution, which gives them a beautiful gloss when dry. In establishments where this is manufactured on a large scale, the liquorice is dissolved in a large bain-marie, and stirred with spatulas which are worked by a steam-engine.

SECTION VIII.—PASTILE DROPS.

CHOOSE the best treble-refined sugar with a good grain, pound it, and pass it through a coarse hair sieve; sift again in a lawn sieve to take out the finest part, as the sugar, when it is too fine, makes the drops heavy and compact, and destroys their brilliancy and shining appearance.

Put some of the coarse grains of sugar into a small drop pan (these are made with a lip on the right side, so that when it is held in the left hand the drops can be detached with the right), moisten it with any aromatic spirit you intend to use, and a sufficient quantity of water to make it of a consistence just to drop off the spoon or spatula without sticking to it. Colour with prepared cochineal, or any other colour, ground fine and moistened with a little water. Let the tint which you give be as light and delicate as possible. Place the pan on the stove fire, on a ring of the same size. Stir it occasionally until it makes a noise, when it is near boiling, *but do not let it boil;* then take it from the fire, and stir it well with the spatula until it is of the consistence that when dropped it will not spread too much, but retain a round form on the surface. If it should be too thin, add a little coarse sugar, which should be reserved for the purpose, and make it of the thickness required. Have some very smooth and even plates, made either of tin or copper; let them be quite clean, and drop them on these, separating the sugar from the lip of the pan with a piece of straight wire, as regularly as possible. About two hours afterwards they may be taken off with a thin knife. If you have not the convenience of tin or copper plates, they may be dropped on smooth cartridge paper. Wet the back of the paper when you want to take them off. Cover the bottom of a sieve with paper, lay them on it, and put them in the stove for a few hours. If they remain too long, it will destroy their fragrancy.

Chocolate Drops. — One pound of sugar, one ounce of chocolate. Scrape the chocolate to a powder, and mix it with the sugar in coarse grains, moisten it with clean water, and proceed according to the instructions already given, but do not mix more than can be dropped out whilst warm at one time. If any remains in the pot, it will grease the next which you mix, and will not attain the consistence required.

Coffee Drops.—One ounce of coffee, one pound of sugar. Make a strong and clear infusion of coffee, as directed for coffee ice, and use it to moisten the sugar. Make the drops as above.

Cinnamon Drops.—One ounce of cinnamon, one pound of sugar. Pulverize the cinnamon, and sift it through a lawn sieve. Mix it with the sugar, and add two or three drops of the essential oil. If the flavour is not strong enough, moisten it with the water and proceed as before. The flavour may be given with the essential oil only colouring them with bole ammoniac.

Clove Drops.—Make as cinnamon.

Vanilla Drops.—Make as cinnamon, using a little sugar to pound the vanilla. Use sufficient to give a good flavour; or it may be moistened with the essence of vanilla; but this greases it as chocolate.

Violet Drops.—One pound of sugar, one ounce of orris-powder. Moisten with water, and colour violet.

Catechu Drops.—One pound of sugar, three ounces of catechu. Make as violet. These may also have the addition of a little musk or ambergris—about fifteen grains.

Ginger Drops.—Mix a sufficient quantity of the best powdered ginger to give it the desired taste, or flavour it with the essence of ginger, and colour it with saffron. Moisten with water, and make as others.

Lemon Drops.—Rub off the yellow rind of some lemons on a piece of rough sugar, scrape it off, and mix it with the coarse sugar. Use sufficient to give a good flavour, and colour with saffron a light yellow; moisten with water, as others.

Rose Drops.—Moisten the sugar with rose water, and colour it with cochineal.

Peppermint Drops.—Moisten the sugar with peppermint water, or flavour it with the essence of peppermint, and moisten it with water.

Orange-flower Drops.—Use orange-flower water to moisten the sugar, or flavour it with the essence of neroli and moisten with water.

Orgeat Drops.—Make milk of almonds, as directed under the head of Orgeat Syrup, using a little orange-flower water; moisten the sugar with it.

Raspberry Drops.—Press out the juice of some ripe raspberries through a piece of flannel or cloth, and moisten the sugar with it. All fruit drops are made in the same way,—that is, with the expressed juice,—except pine-apple. When you first rub off the rind of the fruit on sugar, pound the pulp of the fruit, and pass through a hair sieve. Scrape off the sugar on which the rind was rubbed, and mix it with a sufficient quantity of the pulp to give the desired flavour to the coarse grains, and moisten it with water. The whole of these

grease the sugar, and require the same precautions as chocolate
drops.

SECTION IX.—COMFITS.

A COPPER comfit-pan is requisite for this purpose. A bar, having
chains at each end, with a hook and swivel in the centre, is attached
to it, by which it is suspended from the ceiling or a beam, so as to
hang about as high as the breast over a stove or charcoal fire, that the
pan may be kept at a moderate heat and at such a distance as to
allow it to be swung backwards and forwards without touching the
fire or stove. A preserving-pan, containing clarified syrup, must be
placed by the side of the stove, or over another fire, that it may be
kept hot, but not boiling; also a ladle for throwing the syrup into the
pan, and a pearling cot. This last somewhat resembles a funnel,
without the pipe or tube, and having a small hole in the centre with
a pointed piece of stick or spigot fitted into it, which, being drawn
out a little, allows the syrup when placed in it to run out in a small
stream. A piece of string tied several times across the centre of the
top of the cot, and twisted with the spigot, allows it to be drawn out
and regulated at pleasure.

Scotch Caraway Comfits.—Sift two pounds of seeds in a hair sieve
to free them from dust, put them into the comfit-pan, and rub them
well about the bottom with your hand until they are quite warm; have
some clarified loaf sugar in syrup and boiled to the small thread; give
them a charge by pouring over them about two table-spoonfuls to commence with; rub and shake them well about the pan, that they may
take the sugar equally, until they are quite dry. Be careful in not
making them too wet in the first charges by using too much syrup,
or they will lie of a lump and get doubled, and you will have difficulty in parting them. It will prevent their sticking together if the
hand is passed through them between every swing of the pan, and
also add to their smoothness. Do not let the heat under the pan be
too strong, or it will spoil their whiteness. Give them four or five
charges, increasing the quantity of syrup a little each time, and let
each charge be well dried before another is given, dusting them at
the last charge with flour. Sift them in a hair sieve, and clean the
pan. Put them in again, and give them four or five charges more,
with a dust of flour at the last; then sift them and clean the pan.
Proceed in this manner until they are one-third of the required size.
Put them into the stove or sun to dry until the next day, then clarify
and boil some sugar to the large thread, keep it warm as before, divide
the comfits, and put part of them in the pan, so as not to have too
many at one time, for as they increase in size you must divide them
into convenient portions, so that you may be enabled to work them
properly without encumbering the pan. Give them four or five
charges of syrup, proceeding in the same manner as before, until they

are two-thirds or more of the required size, and stove them until the next day. Continue in this manner with each portion alternately, until they are all done. On the third day, boil the syrup to the small pearl, and give eight or ten charges as before, without using flour, so as to finish them, lessening the quantity of syrup each time. Swing the pan gently, and dry each charge well. Put them in the stove for half an hour or an hour after each charge, and proceed alternately with each portion until they are finished, when they should be about the size of peas. Put them in the stove for a day, then smooth them with the whitest loaf sugar in syrup, boiled to the small thread ; add two or three table-spoonfuls of dissolved gum Arabic with it to give them a gloss. Give three or four charges with a very gentle heat, the syrup being cold and the pan scarcely warm. Work and dry each charge well before another is added : when finished, dry them in a moderate heat. It is the best way, if possible, to dry comfits in the sun, as it bleaches them. If the stove is at a greater heat than the sun in a moderately warm day, which is from 70 to 80 degrees of Fahrenheit, it will spoil their whiteness.

Bath Caraways.—These are made in the same way, but only half the size.

Common Caraways.—Sift the seeds, and warm them in the pan, as for Scotch caraways. Have some gum Arabic dissolved, throw in a ladleful, and rub them well about the pan with the hand until dry, dusting them with flour. Give them three or four coatings in this manner, and then a charge of sugar, until they are about one half the required size. Dry them for a day, give them two or three coatings of gum and flour, finish them by giving three or four charges of sugar, and dry them. These are made about the size of Bath caraways. Colour parts of them different colours, leaving the greatest portion white.

Cinnamon Comfits.—Cinnamon is the bark of a tree, of which there are two sorts. The inferior quality is that usually sold for cinnamon, and is otherwise known as cassia, or *cassia lignea.* This breaks short, and has a slimy mucilaginous taste, is thicker, and of a darker colour than the cinnamon, which is the inner bark. This breaks shivery, and has a warm aromatic taste, and is of a reddish colour.

Take one pound of cinnamon bark, and steep it in water for a few hours to soften it; cut it into small pieces about half an inch long, and the size of a large needle. Dry it in the stove. Put your pieces, when dry, into the comfit-pan, and pour on them a little syrup, as for Scotch caraways, proceeding in the same way until they are one-third the required size. You must not use your hand for these as you would for caraways, as they are liable to break in two. Dry them in the stove, then suspend the pearling pot or cot from the bar of the pan or ceiling, so as to hang over the centre of the pan ; boil some clarified loaf sugar to the large pearl, and fill the cot ; put some of the prepared comfits in the pan, but not too many at a time, as it

47

is difficult to get them to pearl alike.   Keep the syrup at the boiling point: open the spigot of the cot so as to allow it to run in a very small stream, or more like a continued dropping; swing the pan backwards and forwards gently, and keep a stronger fire under the pan than otherwise.   Be careful that the syrup does not run too fast, and wet them too much, but so that it dries as soon as dropped, which causes them to appear rough.   If one cot full of sugar is not enough, put in more until they are the required size.   When one lot is finished put in sieves to dry, and proceed to another; but do not let them lie in the pan after you have finished shaking them.   They will be whiter and better if partly pearled one day and finished the next.   Use the best clarified sugar to finish them.

Coriander Comfits.—Proceed with these as for Scotch caraways, working them up to about the same size.   The next day pearl them to a good size, as for cinnamon.

Celery Comfits.—Put one pound of celery seed into the pan, and proceed as for Scotch caraway comfits, working them up to the size of a large pin's head.   Dry and pearl them as cinnamon.

Caraway Comfits, pearled.—When the comfits are about the size of Bath caraways, dry and pearl them as cinnamon.

Almond Comfits.—Sift some Valencia almonds in a cane or wicker sieve, pick out any pieces of shell which may be amongst them, and also any of the almonds which are either very small or very large, using those which are as near of a size as possible; take about four pounds, put them in the comfit-pan, and proceed in precisely the same way as for Scotch caraways; or, they may first have a coating of dissolved gum Arabic; rub them well about the pan with the hand, and give them a dust of flour; then pour on a little syrup at the small thread, work and dry them well, then give them three or four more charges, and a charge of gum with a dust of flour.   Proceed in this way until they are one-third the required size, then dry them for a day, and proceed and finish as for caraway comfits.   For the cheaper or more common comfits, more gum and flour are used in making them.

Cardamom Comfits.—The seeds should be kept in their husks until they are required to be used, as they lose much of their flavour and virtues when deprived of them.   They are often mixed with grains of paradise, but these have not the aromatic taste of the cardamom, and are more hot and spicy.   Break the husks of the cardamoms by rolling them with a pin; separate the skins from the seeds, put two pounds into the comfit-pan, and proceed as for Scotch caraways. Make them a good size, and quite smooth.

Barberry Comfits.—Pick the barberries from the stalks, and dry them in a hot stove on sieves; when dry, put about two pounds into the comfit-pan, and proceed as for almond comfits, giving them first a charge of gum and flour, and finish as others.   Make them of a good size and quite smooth; finish with very white loaf sugar with syrup.

Cherry Comfits.—These are made from preserved cherries, dried. Roll them in your hand to make them quite round, dust them with powdered loaf sugar, and dry them again; then proceed as for barberry comfits. Any other preserved fruits may be made into comfits after the same manner.

Comfits flavoured with Liqueurs.—Blanch some bitter almonds, or the kernels of apricots or peaches; let them soak in hot water for an hour, then drain them, and put them into any sort of liqueur or spirit you may desire. Lower the strength of the spirit water, that the kernels may imbibe it the better, cork the jug or bottle close, and let them infuse in it until the spirit has fully penetrated them, which will be about fourteen or fifteen days; then take them out, drain and dry them in a moderate heat; when dry, proceed as for almond comfits.

Orange Comfits.—Take some preserved orange-peel, and cut it into small thin strips; dry them in the stove, and make as cinnamon comfits.

Lemon Peel or Angelica may be made into comfits after the same manner. Let the strips of peel be about the size of the pieces of cinnamon, and thoroughly dried before working them in the pan.

Nonpareils.—Pound some loaf sugar, and sift it through a fine wire sieve; sift what has passed through again in a lawn sieve, to take out the finest particles, so that you have only the fine grain of sugar left without dust. Put about two pounds of this into the comfit-pan, and proceed as for Scotch caraways, working them well with the hand until they are about the size of pins' heads.

To colour Nonpareils or Comfits.—Put some of your comfits or nonpareils into the comfit-pan, shake or rub them about until warm, then add a sufficient quantity of prepared liquid colour (see Colours) to give the desired tint; be careful not to make them too wet, nor of too dark a colour, but rather light than otherwise; shake or rub them well about, that they may be coloured equally; dry them a little over the fire, then put them in sieves, and finish drying them in the stove. Clean the pan for every separate colour.

COMFITS IN GUM PASTE.

Raspberry Comfits.—Prepare some gum paste made with sugar, or the scrapings of the comfit-pan pounded and sifted through a lawn sieve. It may be flavoured with raspberry jam, by mixing some with the paste. Colour it with prepared cochineal; mould it into the form of raspberries, and dry them in the stove; when they are perfectly dry and hard, pearl them as for cinnamon comfits, working them until the size of natural raspberries. Colour them when dry with cochineal, as comfits.

Ginger Comfits.—Flavour gum paste with powdered ginger, make it into small balls about the size of coriander seeds, or peas; dry, and proceed as for Scotch caraways. Colour them yellow when finished.

Clove Comfits.—Flavour sugar gum paste with the oil of cloves, and mould it in the form of cloves. Dry and finish as others.

Any flavour may be given to this sort of comfits, and they are moulded to form the article of which it bears the name, or cut into any device with small cutters. Dried, and finished as other comfits.

To colour Loaf-Sugar Dust.—Pound some sugar, and sift it through a coarse hair sieve; sift this again through a lawn sieve, to take out the finer portions. Put the coarse grains into a preserving pan, and warm them over the stove fire, stirring it continually with the hand; pour in some liquid colour to give the desired tint, and continue to work it about the pan until it is dry.

SECTION X.—FRUIT JELLIES.

THESE are the juices of mucilaginous fruits, rendered clear by filtering them through a flannel bag, and adding an equal weight of sugar; boil to the consistence of a jelly. If the boiling is continued too long they will become ropy, or more like treacle.

Apple Jelly.—Take either russet pippins, or any good baking apples; pare and core them, cut them in slices into a preserving pan containing sufficient water to cover them; then put them on the fire, and boil them until they are reduced to a mash. Put it into a hair sieve, that the water may drain off, which you receive in a basin or pan; then filter it through a flannel bag. To every pint of filtered juice add one pound of loaf sugar, clarify, and boil it to the ball. Mix the juice with it, and boil until it jellies; stir it with a spatula or wooden spoon, from the bottom, to prevent burning. When it is boiled enough, if you try it with your finger and thumb, as directed in sugar-boiling, a string may be drawn similar to the small pearl: it may also be known by its adhering to the spatula or spoon, or a little may be dropped on a cold plate; if it soon sets, it is done. Take off the scum which rises on the top. This is in general used for pouring over preserved wet fruits. This jelly may be coloured red with prepared cochineal.

Quince Jelly.—This is made as apple jelly. The seed of the quince is very mucilaginous. An ounce of bruised seed will make three pints of water as thick as the white of an egg.

Red Currant Jelly.—Take three quarts of fine ripe red currants, and four of white; put them into a jar, tie paper over the top, and put them into a cool oven for three or four hours, or else into a pan of boiling water; when they are done, pour them into a jelly bag; what runs out at first put back again; do this until it runs fine and clear. To each pint of filtered juice add one pound of loaf sugar clarified and boiled to the ball: mix the filtered juice with it, and reduce it to a jelly, stirring it well from the bottom with a spatula. What scum forms on the top take off with a skimmer, put it into pots or glasses, and when cold cut some pieces of paper to the size of the tops, steep it in brandy, and put over it; then wet some pieces of bladder, put it over the top of the pot or glass, and tie it down.

White and Black Currant Jelly.—These are made in the same way, using part red currants with the black ones.

Violet-coloured Currant Jelly.—This is made as red currant jelly, mixing two pounds of black currants with ten of red.

Cherry Jelly.—Pick off the stalks and take out the stones of some fine ripe Morello cherries, and to every four pounds of cherries add one pound of red currants; proceed as for currant jelly.

Barberry Jelly.—Take some very ripe barberries, pick them from their stalks, and weigh them. To every pound of fruit take three-quarters of a pound of loaf sugar, add sufficient water to make it into a syrup, put in the barberries, and boil them until the syrup comes to the pearl, taking off any scum which may rise. Then throw them into a fine hair or lawn sieve, and press the berries with a spoon to extract as much juice as possible from them. Receive the syrup and juice in a pan, put it again on the fire, and finish as apple jelly.

Any of these jellies may be made without fire on the same principle as clear cakes. Get the fruit ripe and fresh gathered, obtain the juice by expression, and filter it through a flannel bag; add an equal weight of sugar to that of filtered juice, stir it well together until the sugar is dissolved, and place it in a warm place or the sun for a few days, when it will be a fine jelly. Those made in this manner retain the natural flavour of the fruit.

Raspberry Jelly.—Take one and a half gallons of ripe raspberries and a half gallon of ripe currants, press out the juice and filter it; to a pint of juice add one pound of loaf sugar, and finish as other jellies.

Gooseberry Jelly.—Make as currant jelly; or it may be made of green gooseberries, as apple jelly.

[*Blackberry Jelly.*—Make as currant jelly—using half a gallon of raspberries to one gallon of black currants; finish as usual.]

SECTION XI.—MARMALADES OR JAMS.

MARMALADE is generally a term applied to a preserve made either of oranges, lemons, apples, pears, quinces, or plums; but I know no difference between marmalades and jams, as they are each of them the pulp of fruits reduced to a consistence, with sugar, by being boiled. If it contains too much sugar it will crystallize, or what is termed candy. The top and sides of the vessel which contains it will be covered with a thin coating of sugar; and if there is not enough in it, or it is not sufficiently boiled, it will soon ferment. Keep them in a cool dry place.

Apple Marmalade.—Pare and core some good apples; cut them in pieces into a preserving pan, with sufficient water to cover them; put them on the fire, and boil until they are reduced to a mash, then pass the whole through a colander; to each pound of pulp add twelve ounces of sugar; put it on the fire, and boil it until it will jelly; try it as directed for apple jelly; put it into pots when cold, and cover the top with paper dipped in brandy, or pour over it melted mutton suet, and tie it over with paper or bladder.

Quince Marmalade.—Make as apple, colouring it with prepared cochineal, if required red; let the fruit be quite ripe.

Green Apricot Marmalade or Jam.—Prepare the fruit by blanching and greening (as for green apricots, wet). When they are green, pulp them by rubbing them through a coarse hair sieve or colander; for each pound of pulp clarify and boil to the blow one pound of loaf sugar; mix it with the pulp and boil it until it will jelly; take off any scum which may arise with a skimmer. This jam is of an excellent green colour, and is very useful for ornamenting and piping almond bread, &c.

Cherry Marmalade or Jam.—Take out the stones and stalks from some fine cherries and pulp them through a cane sieve; to every three pounds of pulp add half a pint of currant juice, and three-quarters of a pound of sugar to each pound of fruit; mix together and boil until it will jelly. Put it into pots or glasses.

Currants, raspberries, plums, and gooseberries are all made in the same manner. Pulp the fruit through a cane sieve, the meshes of which are not large enough to admit a currant to pass through whole. To each pound of pulp add one pound of loaf sugar, broken small, and boil to the consistence of a jelly.

Orange Marmalade—Take the same weight of sugar as of oranges; cut the oranges in half, squeeze out the juice, and strain it; boil the peel in water until they are quite tender, and a strong straw may be passed through them; then drain them from the water, scoop out the pulp, leaving the rind rather thin; cut it into thin fillets; boil the juice of the oranges with the sugar, and skim it when it is nearly done; add the peels, and finish as others. Part of the peels may be pounded and mixed with the marmalade, instead of the whole being cut in fillets; but then it is not so clear, and is a practice which is now almost abandoned, except by a few private persons. Lemon marmalade is made in the same way.

[*Grape Marmalade.*—Put green grapes into a preserving pan, with sufficient water to cover them. Put them on the fire and boil until reduced to a mash; put the pulp through a sieve the meshes of which are not sufficiently large to admit the seed to pass through; to each pound of pulp add two pounds of the best loaf sugar and boil to the consistence of a jelly.]

SECTION XII.—OF FRUIT AND OTHER PASTES.

Fruit Pastes and Cakes.—These are the pulp of fruits, reduced by heat to a kind of marmalade, with the addition of from half a pound to a pound, and in some cases, double the weight of sugar to each pound of pulp, which is evaporated to the required consistence. They can be formed into rings, knots, &c., and either crystallized or candied.

Apple or Pippin Paste.—Take any quantity of good dressing apples, pare, core and put them into a preserving pan with a little water, or just sufficient to cover them. Boil until they are reduced to a marmalade, stirring them to prevent burning. To every pound of reduced pulp add half or three-quarters of a pound of loaf sugar, clarified and boiled to the blow; pass the pulp through a hair sieve before you mix the sugar with it; put it on the fire and let it boil for three or four minutes, keeping it constantly stirred from the bottom, when it will be sufficiently evaporated. If it be required coloured, add liquid colour sufficient to give the desired tint when you mix the sugar. Spread the paste on small tin or pewter sheets (these should be about a foot wide, by a foot and a-half long, and perfectly level) with a thin knife, about the eighth of an inch in thickness; put them in the stove for a day; take them out, and cut the paste into long narrow strips, about a quarter of an inch in width; if the paste is dry enough, the strips can be easily pulled off; form them into rings or knots, or cut into diamonds to form leaves, or any other device your fancy may suggest. Put them in boxes with a sheet of paper between each layer. This paste is occasionaly flavoured with lemon, and is principally used for ornamenting the tops of twelfth cakes.

Apple Cheese.—Pare, quarter, and core your apples as for paste; put them into a jar, and cover the top with the parings; tie paper over the top, and bake them in a moderate oven until they are quite done; take off the parings, and pass the apples through a hair-sieve into a preserving pan. To each pound of pulp add half a pound of loaf sugar clarified and boiled to the blow; place it over a slow fire, stirring it constantly from the bottom until reduced to a stiff paste, which will not stick to the hand; put it into small moulds, hoops, or glasses. Dry in a moderately warm stove for a few days; take them out of the moulds, turn them, and place them again in the stove to finish drying. Keep in boxes as paste-knots, or cover the glasses with brandy papers.

Apricot Paste.—Take ripe apricots, put them in a preserving pan with as much water as will cover them; let them simmer on the fire for two or three minutes, or scald until they are tender; drain the water from them, and pass the pulp through a hair sieve; to each pound of pulp take three-quarters of a pound of sugar, which you clarify and boil to the blow; put the apricots on the fire, and let

them simmer, stirring them constantly until reduced to a thick marmalade; then add the sugar; mix it well with the paste, and let it
boil a minute or two longer; take it from the fire, and put into
moulds, pots, or crimped paper cases; or it may be spread on small
plates, as for apple paste, and formed into rings or knots. Place in
the stove until dry. If put in paper cases, the paper must be wetted
to get out the paste. Take it out of the moulds, turn it, and put it
again into the stove to finish drying.

Green Apricot Paste.—Take apricots before they are ripe, scald as
the last, and green them. (See Greening Fruit.) Pass the pulp
through a sieve, and reduce it; to each pound of reduced pulp add
one pound of loaf sugar clarified and boiled to the blow. Finish as
ripe apricot paste.

Currant Paste.—Put any quantity of ripe currants, either red or
white, or a part of each mixed, into a hair sieve, press out their juice
into a preserving pan; put it on the fire, and keep it constantly stirred until evaporated to a thick consistence. To each pound of reduced pulp add three-quarters of a pound or a pound of loaf sugar
clarified and boiled to the blow. Let it boil a minute or two, and
finish as others.

Black Currant Paste is made the same as the last. These currants,
not being so juicy as the others, may be put into a jar, tied over, and
baked in a moderate oven, or put into a kettle of boiling water for a
few hours, to extract the juice from them.

Raspberry Paste.—As currant paste.

Cherry Paste.—Take ripe cherries, deprive them of their stalks
and stones, put them in a preserving pan, and boil them a little; then
pass them through a hair sieve, reduce the pulp, and weigh it. To
each pound add a pound of loaf sugar; add it to the paste, and finish
as apricot.

Peach Paste.—Choose some very fine and ripe peaches, take off the
skin, and cut them in small pieces into a preserving pan; put them
on the fire, and reduce to a thick consistence, stirring it continually.
For each pound of reduced pulp take half or three-quarters of a
pound of sugar; clarify and boil it to the blow; add it to the pulp;
put it again on the fire, and let it boil a few minutes. Finish as
other pastes.

Plum Paste.—Plums of any kind are preserved in the same manner, whether green-gages, magnum-bonums, Orleans, damsons, &c.
Take out their stones, and boil the fruit in a little water, as for apricot paste; pass them through a sieve, and for each pound of reduced
pulp take a pound of sugar; clarify and boil it to the blow; mix it
with the paste, and evaporate to the required consistence.

Damson Cheese.—Pick the stalks from the damsons, put them in a
jar, tie it over, and bake in a cool oven; when done, pass them
through a sieve into a preserving pan; put it on the fire to reduce.

For each pound of pulp take half a pound of sugar, boiled to the blow; mix with the paste, and finish as for apple cheese. This, as well as all the pastes, may be evaporated to the required consistence by means of a water bath, which is done by placing the pan in which it is contained in another with water, which is kept boiling; this prevents the possibility of its being burnt, but it occupies more time. The kernels of the fruit may be blanched and added to it just before it is taken from the fire. Put it into moulds or hoops; dry them in the stove, first on one side and then on the other. All plums are done in the same manner.

Quince Paste.—Proceed as for apple paste.

Orange Paste.—Squeeze the juice from Seville or sweet oranges, and boil the peels in three or four waters to take off part of their bitterness. In the first put a little salt. When they are quite tender remove the white pith or pulp, and pound them quite fine in a mortar, with part of the juice, using sufficient to make them into a paste; then pass it and the remaining portion of the juice through a sieve into a preserving pan; put it on the fire, and reduce to a marmalade; weigh it, and for each pound take three-quarters of a pound of loaf sugar; clarify and boil to the blow; mix it with the paste, evaporate over a gentle fire to a good consistence, and finish as apple. The rinds of the oranges may be pared off before they are squeezed, which, if boiled in one water, will be sufficient, as the pith of the peel is extremely bitter and indigestible, and the flavour or essential oil is contained only in the yellow porous part.

Lemon Paste.—Make as orange paste, using part of the juice and double the weight of sugar; or it may be made by using only the pounded peel with the same weight of sugar.

Raspberry Cakes.—Take ripe raspberries, press the juice from half of them, and put the pulp back with the others; reduce them on the fire. To each pound of pulp add two pounds of loaf sugar in powder; put it again on the fire, stirring it constantly until it is evaporated to a very thick paste. Have a tin ring, with a handle by the side, about the size of an old penny piece, and twice the thickness; wet the ring, and place it on your small pewter or tin plates, fill it with the paste, smoothing over the top with a knife; then remove the ring, and the cake will remain. Lay them off in rows, and make three or four marks on the top with the handle of a table spoon; put them in the stove to dry, turn them with a thin knife, and put them again in the stove to dry perfectly. Place them in boxes, with paper between each layer.

The residue from the making of raspberry vinegar may be employed for this purpose, or they may be made by adding a pound of fine powdered sugar to a pound of jam. Any of the fruit pastes may be formed into cakes like these, or into drops, by forcing them out on paper with a small pipe and bladder attached to it.

Clear Cakes, or Jelly Cakes. — Take the filtered juice of fruits, as for jelly (see Jellies); to each pint of juice add one pound of loaf sugar, dissolve it in the juice thoroughly, place it on the fire and heat it, but it must not boil; put it into small pots, moulds, or glasses, so as to form cakes about half an inch thick; place them on the stove, which must not be too hot, or they will melt instead of forming a jelly; about seventy-five or eighty degrees Fahrenheit is quite hot enough.   When a crust has formed on the top, take out the cakes by carefully turning the knife round the sides of the pot, place them on small plates of tin or pewter, and dry on the other side.   When dry they can be cut into diamonds, squares, or any shape you please. These are certainly some of the most delicate and beautiful of this class which were ever invented, fit even to gratify the palate of the most fastidious.   The fruit from which they are made should be gathered as fresh as it possibly can, except apples, as the mucilage is injured by keeping, and if the fruit has fermented it is entirely destroyed.

Pastes formed with Gum — Pâte de Guimauve — Marsh-Mallow Paste. — Gum Arabic three pounds, roots of fresh marsh-mallows eight ounces, one dozen of rennet apples, loaf sugar three pounds. Peel, core, and cut the apples in pieces. Cleanse the roots, and slice them lengthways in an oblique direction; add this to seven pints of water; soft or river-water is the best when filtered; put it on the fire and boil for a quarter of an hour, or until reduced to six pints; pound and sift the gum through a hair sieve; strain the decoction into a pan with the gum; put it on a moderate fire, or into a bain-marie, stirring it until the gum is perfectly dissolved; then strain it through a coarse towel or tamis cloth, the ends being twisted by two persons; add it to the sugar, which has been previously clarified and boiled to the feather; dry it well over the fire, keeping it constantly stirred from the bottom. When it has acquired a thick consistence, take the whites of eighteen eggs, and whip them to a strong froth; add them to the paste, and dry until it does not stick to the hand when it is applied to it; add a little essence of neroli, or a large glassful of double orange-flower water, and evaporate again to the same consistence. Pour it on a marble slab well dusted with starch-powder, flatten it with the hand; the next day cut it into strips, powder each strip, and put them in boxes. Powder the bottom that they may not stick.

Pâte de Gomme Arabique—Arabic Paste.—Very white gum Arabic two pounds, sugar two pounds, orange-flower water four ounces, the whites of twelve eggs. Pound and sift the gum, add it to the water, dissolve and evaporate it over a slow fire, or in the bain-marie, stirring it constantly until it is reduced to the consistence of honey with the sugar in syrup. Whip the whites to a strong snow; add it to the paste with the orange-flower water, gradually; stir and finish as marsh-mallow paste, for which this is mostly substituted, and much used for coughs. It should be very white, light, and spongy.

Pâte des Dattes—Date Paste.—Dates one pound, gum Senegal three pounds, loaf sugar in syrup two pounds and a half, orange-flower water four ounces. Make as marsh-mallow paste, using rather more water to dissolve the gum.

Pâte des Jujubes—Jujube Paste.—Jujubes four ounces, currants washed and picked four ounces, raisins stoned one pound, sugar two pounds, very white gum Arabic two pounds and a half. Open the jujubes, and boil them with the currants and raisins in two quarts of water until reduced to three pints, strain the decoction through a tamis cloth, twisted by two persons; add the sugar in syrup with the gum, which has been previously pounded and dissolved in a sufficient quantity of water; evaporate it by a moderate heat, as pâte de gui-mauve; pour it into tin moulds slightly oiled, having edges about a quarter of an inch deep; dry in the stove, take it out of the tins, and cut it with a pair of scissors into small diamonds.

Pâte de Gomme Senegal—Senegal Paste.—Gum Senegal two pounds, sugar one pound. Dissolve the gum in orange-flower water and common water; or dissolve it in common water, and flavour with essence of neroli; add the sugar, when clarified and boiled to the blow; evaporate, and finish as pâte de jujube. This is usually sold for jujube paste, or else picked gum Arabic made into a paste as Senegal, and coloured with prepared cochineal or saffron.

Pâte de blanche Réglisse,— White Liquorice Paste.—This is made the same as marsh-mallow paste, using liquorice-root instead of mallow. It may be made without the eggs, and finished as jujubes.

Pâte de Réglisse noir — Black Liquorice Paste.—The best refined liquorice one pound, gum Arabic four pounds, loaf sugar two pounds, Florence orris-root one ounce. Dissolve the gum and liquorice in seven pints of water, keeping it stirred over a slow fire; add the sugar in syrup with the orris-root, evaporate to a paste, and finish as jujubes.

Gomme des Jujubes—Jujube Gum.—Jujubes one pound, very white and picked gum Arabic two pounds, powdered sugar two ounces. Pound the jujubes in a marble mortar with five pints of water, put the whole into a pan and boil until reduced to three; strain the decoction through a cloth, beat up the white of an egg with a glass of water, and mix part of it with the decoction as it boils; throw in a little at a time of the remaining part, to check the ebullition. When it is all used, take off the scum, put it again on the fire to evaporate the water, adding at the same time the gum and sugar, powdered and passed through a horse-hair sieve. Stir it with the spatula until dissolved. When it is of the consistence of honey, place it in the bain-marie, and neither stir nor touch it, that it may be clear. When it has acquired body enough, so as not to stick to the back of the hand when applied to it, pour it into moulds previously oiled with good olive oil, as for jujubes; place in the stove to finish drying; when dry take it out, and cut in small pieces.

Pâte de jujube and white liquorice may be done in the same manner, using only half the quantity of sugar.

Gomme des Dattes.—One pound of dates, two pounds of very white picked gum Arabic, sugar two ounces. Make as jujubes.

Gum of Violets.—Violet flowers one pound, picked gum two pounds, sugar four ounces in syrup. Pour three pints of water at the boiling point on the flowers in an earthen jar; stop it perfectly close, and keep it in a warm place for ten or twelve hours; strain the infusion by expression into a flat pan or dish, place it on an inclination, and let it rest for an hour that the fæces may subside; pour off the clear gently from the bottom or settling, and add to it six grains of turnsole bruised, and six grains of carmine, as this clear infusion is not sufficiently coloured to give it the beautiful tint of the violet. Mix in the powdered gum and sugar, stir it over a moderate fire until dissolved, pass it through a sieve, and finish in the bain-marie as jujubes.

Any of these gums, when dry, may be crystallized.

Almond Paste— Orgeat Paste. — One pound of sweet almonds, a quarter of a pound of bitter almonds, two pounds of sugar. Blanch the almonds, and throw them into clean cold water as they are done, to preserve their whiteness; let them soak for a day, then dry them in a cloth, and pound them quite fine in a mortar, sprinkling them with orange-flower water or lemon juice to prevent their oiling; then with a spatula rub them through a fine wire sieve; what will not pass through, pound again until they are quite fine; clarify the sugar and boil it to the ball; mix the almonds with it, and stir it well over the fire with the spatula until it comes together; then take it from the fire, and put it into an earthen pan to cool; when cold, pound it again, make it into sticks or tablets, dusting the board or stone with powdered sugar; or put into pots, and tie bladder over it, to be used as wanted.

SECTION XIII.—FRUITS PRESERVED WITH SUGAR.

WET FRUITS. — Most of the fruits are first prepared by being blanched, that is, boiled in water; they are then drained and put into boiling syrup, where they remain for a day. The syrup being now weakened with the juice of the fruit, it is poured off, more sugar is added, and it is reduced again to syrup by boiling, and poured hot over the fruit: this is continued until it is fully saturated with sugar, which may be known by the syrup being no longer weakened with the juice of the fruit. Keep them in a dry but not warm place, as too much heat will cause them to ferment, more especially if they are not fully incorporated with sugar; nor in a damp place, or they will become mouldy.

All green fruits require to be greened, so as to bring them to their original colour, for in blanching they assume a yellowish cast: this is probably occasioned by a portion of the alkali being extracted in the ooiing. The green colour of fruits and leaves depends upon an excess of alkali; and in proportion as acid or alkali prevails in them, so are they coloured from red to violet, blue, and green; therefore if alkali is added to the water, the colour is retained. This is exemplified in the everyday domestic duties of the cook, who uses soda, potash, or muriate of soda (common salt), in boiling her greens or cabbages. I have here stated the principle on which their colour depends, to show that there is no necessity for green fruits being kept for some time in brass or copper pans, whereby they take up a portion of verdigris, which often proves injurious.

Prick your fruit several times with a fork or large needle, to allow the sugar to penetrate the more freely. As you do them, throw them into a pan of cold water, which prevents their turning black at the places where they are pricked; add a little soda or potash, and set the pan by the side of the stove to heat gradually, but not to boil, or at the most only to simmer; when the fruit swims, take it out with a skimmer and put it into cold water; if they are not green enough, drain them and put them again into the water they were first boiled in, or else into a weak syrup; place them by the side of the stove to heat gradually as before, stirring them occasionally. They may be covered with vine leaves, or a handful of spinach; if salt is used in greening them, they will require to be soaked for a few hours in clean cold water, to again extract that portion which they have absorbed, or it will spoil their flavour. It is best to blanch fruits which are very juicy in hard or pump water, or with the addition of a little alum to river water.

Green Apricots, wet.—Get the apricots before the stone is formed in them, when they can be pierced through with a pin or needle; put them into a bag with plenty of salt, and shake them about in it to take off the down and silkiness of the skin; take them out and put them in cold water. Or this may be done by making a strong ley with wood ashes; strain it through a cloth; let it be quite clear; make it boiling hot and throw in your apricots; let them remain about a minute, take them out, and put them into cold water; then take off the fur when they are cool by either rubbing them with your hands in the water, or drain, and rub them in a towel or coarse cloth. Put them into another pan of cold water, and place them over a slow fire to heat gradually and scald. When they are quite soft and can be crushed between the finger and thumb, take them out and throw them into cold water; drain them quite dry in sieves; make a thin syrup, that is, at the small thread; boil it in a flat preserving pan, put in the apricots, give them a few boils, and take off any scum that rises; have sufficient syrup in the pan that the fruit may float; pour them with the syrup into an earthen pan, and keep them covered until the next day; then drain off the syrup, add more syrup or sugar to it, and boil to the large thread; put in the fruit, and let the syrup boil over them four or five times: repeat these operations for five days, increasing the syrup a degree each day until it has attained the large pearl, taking off the scum each time: it must not exceed this, or it will crystallize; put them in dry pans covered with syrup, for use; or, when cold, drain them from the syrup, and put them into small glasses by themselves, or mixed with other fruits preserved in the same manner; fill the vacancies with apple jelly, wet a piece of bladder and tie it over the top.

Green Apricots, pared wet. — Pare off the skin with a small knife, and throw them into cold water as you do them; green, and finish as the former.

Ripe Apricots, wet. — Have the fruit not too ripe, make an incision in the side to take out the stone, or they may be cut in halves, and peeled or preserved with the skin on; have a preserving pan on the fire with water boiling, throw them in, and as they rise to the top take them out and put them into cold water. If they are blanched too much they will break, therefore it is better to have two pans of cold water to throw them in, so as those may be separated which are broken; drain them from the water, and put them in a thin syrup which is boiling on the fire; do not put in too many at a time; put in the hardest first, and give them about a dozen boils; take them out carefully and put them in an earthen pan; give the soft ones only two or three boils; cover them with the syrup and let them remain until the next day; drain the syrup from them, add more sugar to it, and boil and skim it until it has acquired the degree of the large thread; give the apricots two or three boils in it; the soft ones only require to have the syrup poured on them boiling hot; repeat this for four or five successive days, and on the last day boil the syrup to the large pearl. If you find, after they are finished, that the syrup has been boiled too high, mix a little powdered alum with a spoonful of water, and add to it.

Ripe Peaches, whole, wet. — Get the finest peaches, without any green spots on the skin; prick them all over with a large needle to the stone, throw them into cold water, blanch, and finish as ripe apricots.

Ripe Nectarines, wet.—Preserve as peaches.

Figs, wet.—Get the figs nearly ripe, prick them four or five times with the point of a knife, throw them into cold water, put them on the fire and boil until they are tender; finish as ripe apricots.

Greengages, wet.—Let the fruit be not quite ripe but sound, prick them with a fork or needle, and throw them into cold water; scald and green them; when they are of a fine green, increase the heat; take them out with a skimmer when they swim, and throw them into cold water; drain them on sieves; put them in syrup that is boiling; give them two or three boils in it; pour them into an earthen pan; drain the syrup from them the next day, add more sugar and boil to the thread, taking off any scum which may arise; pour the syrup over them boiling hot; repeat this for five or six days, and finish as for green apricots.

Mogul Plums.—Take the largest Mogul plums, with clear skins, not quite ripe, prick them all over with a fork and throw them into cold spring water; scald them until tender, taking care not to have too many in the pan at a time, nor blanch them too much, as they will soon break in pieces; take them out and throw them into cold water, drain, and put in just sufficient fruit to cover the bottom of the pan; cover with boiling syrup, and let them have a dozen boils in it; finish as ripe apricots.

It would be a needless repetition, to give separate directions for preserving every sort of plum, as the instructions already given will enable any person of ordinary discernment to manage any other sort not mentioned.

Damsons, wet.—Prick the damsons and throw them into boiling syrup, and let them boil in it until the skins burst, skimming it as they boil; do not put in any more than will swim; let them remain until the next day; drain the syrup, and add more sugar to bring it to the proper degree; give them a few boils in it, and repeat the same on the next day; finish as other plums.

Green Gooseberries, wet.—Get some fine large gooseberries, prick them three or four times with a large needle, and throw them into cold water; put them on the fire to blanch; when they rise take them out and throw them into cold water, green them, and preserve as green apricots.

Green Gooseberries in the form of Hops, wet—Take the finest green gooseberries for this purpose, slit each gooseberry in four or six slits, but so as not to come asunder, and take out the seeds. Take a needle and white thread, make a knot at the end, and pass the needle through the stalk end of the gooseberry that is split; take another and do the same, making the end of one go partly into the other; continue this until you have six or eight on the thread, which will resemble a hop; fasten the end of the thread, and dispose of all of them in the same manner, throwing them into cold water as they are finished: blanch them, and let them lie in the water they were blanched in all night; the next day green them, and finish as for green gooseberries, wet.

Cucumbers or Gherkins, wet.—Let them be clear, free from all spots, and of a good green; prick them all over with a fork, throw them into a pan of water mixed with a handful of salt, let them lie in this for a day or two, then take them out, put them into fresh water and blanch them until tender; the next day drain and green them in a weak syrup; increase the degree of the syrup each day, giving them a few boils in it each time; if the cucumbers are large, you can cut them in two and take out the seeds. After the second boiling in the syrup, let them remain in it for two or three days before it is boiled again: finish as green apricots; a few pieces of ginger may be added.

Green Melons.—Proceed as for cucumbers. They may be preserved either whole or in slices. When dried and candied, it imitates green citron.

Ripe Melons, wet.—Cut the melons in slices, and pare off the outside skin ; let them lie in salt and water for two or three days, take them out, drain and blanch in fresh water until tender ; throw them into cold water; when cold, drain them on sieves; give them a boil in thin syrup the next day, increase the degree of the syrup, and pour it boiling hot over them. A little lemon-juice, vinegar, or a handful of bruised ginger may be added to the syrup, which will much improve the flavour; boil the syrup, increasing it a degree for three or four days, as for other fruits.

Lemons whole, wet. — Choose some fine large lemons with clear skins, carve the rind with a small penknife, into flowers, stars, diamonds, or any design your fancy may suggest, taking care not to cut deeper than the white pith of the peel ; throw them into a pan of cold water, put them on the fire and let them boil gently until a strong straw or the head of a pin will penetrate the rind ; throw them into cold water; when cold, drain them dry, and put them into a thin syrup when boiling ; give them five or six boils in it, and put them in an earthen pan . the next day drain the syrup from them, and add more sugar or syro to increase it a degree ; boil it and when it boils, pour it over th lemons: repeat this for two days; on the third day let the lemons boil in the syrup for four or five minutes; the next day boil the syrup and pour it over them; when you find the syrup has penetrated the lemons, and they look clear, drain the syrup from them, adding more if necessary, so as to have sufficient to keep them well covered; put them in glasses, and pour the syrup over them. When cold, cut a piece of bladder to the size of the glass, wet it, and tie it down.

Oranges whole, wet.—These are preserved the same as lemons.

Whole Orange Peels.—Choose your oranges of a fine clear skin; make a hole at the stalk end, large enough to admit the end of a spoon, with which you take out the pulp; throw them in salt and water, and let them remain for three or four days or a week ; drain them from this, and put them into a pan of fresh water, and let them boil until the end of a straw may be pushed through the peel ; throw them into cold water; with the end of a spoon clear out any part of the pulp which may have adhered to them ; drain off the water ; put them in a tub or pan, and pour boiling syrup over them; let them remain in this for three or four days; take them from the syrup and boil it again, adding more as the peels imbibe it, so as to keep them well covered; boil the syrup once every four or five days, and pour it hot over them; do this until it has fully penetrated them.

Orange or Lemon Peels, wet.—Cut the fruit in half; express the juice, and throw the peels into salt and water, as for whole orange peels, preserving them in the same way. If you have any quantity, put them one in the other, and pack them in rows round the bottom of a large tub or cask ; proceed in this manner, putting them in layers until it is half or three parts full ; have a hole near the bottom, with a cork fitted into it. When the syrup requires boiling, draw it off at the hole.

Orange or Lemon Chips.—Cut the thickest peels into long thin pieces, turning them off so as to make but one or two chips from a peel, in a similar manner as you would pare off the rind of an apple, only, instead of holding the knife in an oblique direction, so as to take off the surface, it is held more parallel, so as to cut the whole substance of the peel. Let them be as near as possible of the same thickness, or the peel may be sliced across, so as to form rings; preserve them as for whole orange peels. If they are wanted in a hurry, they may be blanched without being put into salt and water. Boil them until they can be crushed between the finger and thumb; drain them from the water, and pour boiling syrup over them as for others.

Angelica, wet.—Cut some stalks of fine tender angelica into pieces about six inches long, or any other suitable length. Put them into a pan of water on the fire until they are soft, then put them into cold water ; draw off the skin and strings with a knife, and put them into cold water again ; next boil them until they look whitish ; let them cool ; drain them from the water, and put them in an earthen pan ; pour boiling syrup over them until they float. The next day drain it off, without disturbing the angelica ; boil with more sugar, if required, taking off any scum which may rise ; pour it over the stalks whilst it is hot ; repeat this for seven or eight days, boiling the syrup the last time to the large pearl.

Eringo Root.—Choose your roots without knots; wash them clean, and boil in water until they are tender ; peel off the outside skin, slit them, take out the pith, and throw them into cold water ; drain, put them into a thin syrup, and give them a few boils ; afterwards finish as angelica.

Pine Apple whole, wet. — Take off the top and stem of the pine ; prick the apple with a pointed knife in six or eight places, or more, to the centre ; put the pine in a pan with plenty of water, and boil it until tender ; take it out and throw it into cold water ; when cold, drain it quite dry, and pour over it, boiling hot, some syrup at the small thread. In two days pour off the syrup and boil it to a degree higher, adding more sugar if necessary ; repeat this every third day, until the pine is sufficiently impregnated with the sugar ; the last time the sugar must be at the large pearl. The top of the pine is greened and preserved as other green fruits, putting it in its proper place when finished. Carefully skim the sugar each time, that the pine may be quite clear.

Pine Apple Chips or Slices. — Take off the top and stalk, and pare the outside of the pine ; cut it into slices half an inch thick ; strew over the bottom of a pan with powdered sugar ; cover it with slices of pine-apple, then a layer of sugar, and again of pine, and so alternately until the whole is disposed of, covering the top with a layer of sugar; place it in a warm place or stove for three or four days; then boil it with the juice of two or three lemons for ten minutes or a quarter of an hour, taking off any scum which rises. If the syrup is too thick, add a little water; continue this boiling for three or four days, when it will be fit for use.

Cherries, wet or dry. — Take the best Kentish or May Duke cherries; cut a quill as if you were going to make a pen, only, instead of its being sharp, it must be round at the end; hold the cherry in your left hand, and with the other push the quill into it by the side of the stalk, as far as the top of the stone; then take hold of the stalk, and with the aid of the quill pull the stone out with the stalk, without breaking the fruit in pieces, which would be the case otherwise. Put sufficient clarified sugar into a preserving pan for the cherries to swim; boil it to the blow, and throw in the prepared fruit; let them boil in it for five or ten minutes, keeping them under the syrup by pushing them down with a flat piece of wood having a handle at the back. The next day drain off the syrup; reduce it by boiling; put in the cherries and boil them again for five minutes; repeat this for four days, giving the cherries a few boils in the syrup each day. If they are required dry, drain the syrup from them, spread them on sieves, and dry in the stove at a good heat, turning them every day. Put only sufficient on the sieves so as just to cover the bottom. Keep them in boxes prepared, or in glasses.

Whole Cherries. — Shorten the stalks of some fine cherries; put them into an earthen pan, with a layer of powdered sugar and a layer of cherries, covering the top with sugar; let them stand for two or three days; put them on the fire in a preserving pan, and let them boil in the syrup for three or four minutes; repeat this for four days. Keep them in syrup, or dry, when they are wanted, as the preceding; they may also be tied together to form bunches, and preserved in the same manner.

Grapes in Bunches. — Get some bunches of fine grapes, before they are perfectly ripe; take out the stones with a large pin or needle; put them in a preserving pan, with plenty of water and a little salt; let them simmer on the fire about a quarter of an hour; cover the pan, and let them stand in this water until the next day; pour this off, and add fresh; in a few hours drain them dry, and put them into a thin syrup, which must be boiling on the fire; give them a few boils in it, or the grapes may be put into the syrup when cold, and heat it gradually until it boils; put them in an earthen pan; the next day drain off the syrup, reduce it to the small pearl, adding more sugar if necessary, and skimming it; pour it boiling over the grapes; repeat this four or five times, finishing with syrup at the large pearl, and keep them well covered in it.

Currants in Bunches, wet. — Take the finest currants you can get, either red or white; stone them with a pin or the nib of a pen, taking care not to cut them more than is necessary; tie six or eight bunches together with a piece of thread, or they may be tied to a small piece of stick. Take as much clarified sugar as will allow the currants to float; or put one pound of sugar to each pound of currants; clarify and boil it to the blow; put in your fruit, and let them have five or six boils; take the scum off with paper; repeat the boiling next day when they are finished. If you boil them again, the syrup will become a jelly, when you can put them in glasses.

Barberries in Bunches, wet.—Proceed as for currants.

Raspberries, whole, wet.—Take the finest and driest raspberries you can get, but not over-ripe. Take the same quantity of sugar in weight as you have of raspberries; clarify and boil it to the blow; put in the fruit, and give them a dozen boils, taking off the scum with paper; drain off the syrup, and put them into pots that are very dry; cover them with apple jelly, or make a jelly with the syrup the raspberries were boiled in, with the addition of a little currant or cherry juice when cold. Tie them over with brandy papers and bladder.

Pears, whole, wet.—Take some fine large pears, either eating or baking, but those for eating must not be too ripe; they are fit for this purpose when the pips are black. Throw them into a pan of water, with two ounces of alum; put them on the fire, and scald them until tender; take them out, and throw them into cold water; pare off the rind very thin and even; prick them several times with a fork or pin to the core, and scald them again until they are quite soft, or until the head of a pin or straw will pass through them; a little lemon juice may be added to the water in the second boiling, or with the syrup; when they are finished blanching, throw them into cold water; when cold drain them from this, and put them into a thin syrup at the small thread; give them two or three boils in this; skim, and put them in an earthen pan; the next day drain off the syrup, and add more sugar, and reduce it another degree; boil your pears in it, as before, and repeat the process for four days, finishing with the syrup at the large pearl. Keep them in covered pans for use.

Pears, Red, wet.—Take some good baking or other pears; pare and cut them in half, and take out the cores with a little scoop for the purpose; if they are first blanched a little, they can be pared easier and better. Boil them in water, with sugar sufficient to make it only just sweet, a little lemon juice, and a few allspice or cloves. Put a piece of pewter, or a pewter spoon, in the bottom of the pan, and boil them until they are quite tender and of a fine red; or prepared cochineal may be added instead, using sufficient to give the desired tint; take out the fruit, and add enough sugar to the water they were boiled in to make a syrup; boil to the large thread; put in the pears, and give them two or three boils in it; skim, and put them in an earthen pan; boil the syrup twice more, and pour it on them, raising it to the degree of the large pearl. Keep them in dry pans for use

Quinces, Red or White, wet.—Preserve as pears.

For these preserves it is a good plan to have flat pieces of wood, like covers, to put on the fruit, so as to keep it under the syrup.

Ginger, wet.—This article is mostly imported from India and China, in jars or pots. Divide the largest races or roots from the smaller ones; take largest for preserving, as the smaller ones will serve for planting; clean and cut the roots into neat pieces, and throw them into cold water as you do them. Boil them three times in fresh water, throwing them into cold each time, or soak them in water for four or five days; drain, and boil in fresh water till tender; take them out, and throw them into cold water, in which has been mixed a little lemon juice or vinegar; peel them, and throw them into the water again as they are done, to keep them white; let the roots remain in this a few hours, then drain them dry on sieves; put them in an earthen pan; pour over them, when cold, a thin syrup, at the small thread; let them be well covered with the syrup; in two or three days drain off the syrup; add more sugar, and boil to the large thread; when cold pour it over the ginger. After three or four days boil the sugar a degree higher, and pour it in hot; continue this until your roots look clear and are fully impregnated with sugar; finish with the syrup at the large pearl.

Candied Fruit.—Any fruit or peel which has been first preserved in syrup may be candied.

Take the fruit out of the syrup and let it drain on sieves; then dip the sieve with the fruit into lukewarm water, to wash off the syrup from the surface; take it out, let it drain, and dry it in the stove. Boil some fresh syrup to the blow; put in the fruit and give it a boil in it. The fruit when it is put in will reduce the sugar, it must therefore be boiled to the same degree again. With a spoon or spatula rub the sugar against the side of the pan, to grain it; when it begins to whiten put the fruit in the white part separately: with two forks take it out and lay it on sieves or wire frames, for the sugar to drain from it.

Dried Fruit.—Any of those fruits which are preserved with syrup may be dried: they are also better when fresh dried. Warm the fruit in the syrup; take it out and drain; spread it on sieves or wires; put them in the stove to dry, turning them frequently until perfectly dried. When the fruit is drained from the syrup, it may be dusted with loaf-sugar when you put it in the stove, and for two or three times when you turn it. Too much heat will blacken the fruit, therefore let the heat of the stove be about 100° or 110° of Fahrenheit's thermometer.

SECTION XIV.—COMPOTES.

THESE are prepared in the same way as wet fruits, and served in compotiers, which are deep glass dishes belonging to the dessert service.

In summer, ripe fruits are simply blanched and boiled up in a thin syrup, a little lemon-juice is added, and served; these are only for present use. In winter, take those fruits which are preserved in syrup, drain, dip them in luke-warm water, and serve in a thin syrup, with the juice of a lemon.

Green Apricot Compote.—Prepare your fruit as for green apricots, wet; throw them into syrup that is boiling; take them off the fire, and let them remain for four or five hours; drain off the syrup, and boil to the thread; pour it over the fruit; when cold, serve.

Ripe Apricot Compote.—Cut the apricots in half, and peel them; blanch them in water that is just sweetened; drain them from this; add sugar to the water, and boil to the thread; pour it over the apricots; let them remain in it for two or three hours; then drain and boil the syrup again to the large thread; pour it over the apricots; add the juice of a lemon, with some of the kernels blanched; when cold, serve.

Peaches, nectarines, and green-gages are done as these.

Compote of Apples, with Jelly.—Pare some fine pippins very neatly; core them with an apple corer; put them into syrup, and boil gently; put only just sufficient syrup to cover them, that it may be reduced to a jelly; if it has not body enough, cut a few in pieces and put with it; when the apples look clear and are tender, take them out; add to the apples, while boiling, the juice and yellow rind of a lemon, with a few cloves. Strain the syrup, and reduce it to a jelly; pour part into the compotier, and when cold dress the apples tastefully on it. The hole where the core was taken out may be filled with any sort of marmalade or jelly. Cut the remaining part of the jelly in pieces or croutons, and place round or over them; ornament them with red currant or other jelly, in any way that your fancy may dictate.

Apple Compote.—Take some fine apples; peel and cut them in halves, quarters, or thick slices, and take out the cores; blanch them in a very thin syrup until tender; take them out, and add more sugar to that which they were boiled in, with the yellow peel and juice of a lemon and a few cloves; reduce it to the small pearl; put in the apples, and give them a few boils in it; let them remain until cold; take off the scum, if any; strain the syrup, and serve.

Pears and quinces are done as these, or coloured as for pears wet, which see.

Grape Compote.—Pick and stone some fine ripe grapes; put them in boiling syrup at the large pearl; give them three or four boils in it; let them cool, take off the scum, and serve.

Currant Compote.—Take the largest currants you can get, either red or white; pick out the seeds, and throw them into boiling syrup at the large pearl; give them two or three boils, and let them stand in the syrup; take off the scum, and serve when cold.

Raspberry Compote.—Choose some very fine and dry raspberri⸱ boil some syrup to the blow, take it from the fire, and throw in ʰᵗ raspberries; let them stand for four or five hours; stir them gently; put them on the fire, and let the syrup just boil; take off the scum, and when cold serve.

Strawberry Compote.—Take off the stalks, and throw them into syrup at the small thread; when it is near boiling, take them off, let them cool, and serve; or they may be prepared by putting them in the compotier, and covering them with white currant jelly warmed.

Macedoine of Fruits.—Put some of all sorts of fruits, prepared for compotes, together, and serve in the same glass, with syrup and a little lemon-juice.

Cherry Compote.—Cut off the stalks of some fine cherries about half way; wash them in cold water, and let them drain quite dry; boil some syrup to the large pearl; throw in the cherries, and let them boil quickly for five or six boils; take them off, and let them remain until cold; take off the scum, if any, and, dress them in the compotier, with their stalks upwards; pour in the syrup, and serve, adding the juice of lemon.

Damsons, mulberries, Orlean plums, and barberries are done the same way, taking out the stones of the plums and barberries; the cherries may be also stoned.

SECTION XV.—BRANDY FRUITS⸱

ALL fruits may be preserved with brandy; but only the best sort of plums, such as apricots, magnum-bonums, peaches, green-gages, mirabelles, &c., with cherries and pears, are those usually done.

The fruit should be gathered before it is perfectly ripe, when it is prepared by blanching, &c., precisely the same as if it were intended for wet fruits; those preserved in this manner are often taken from their syrup and put in brandy; when the fruits are blanched put them for a day or two in a thin syrup, then take them out and arrange them in glasses; cover them with white brandy, into which you have mixed five ounces of powdered white sugar candy, and tie them over with bladder. Cherries are an exception to this rule. Take some fine Morello cherries, and cut off half the stalk; put them into brandy, and stop them close for a month; drain off the brandy, and to each quart add eight ounces of powdered loaf sugar or white sugar candy; dissolve and pour it over the cherries. Keep them well covered with spirit.

SECTION XVI.—ON BOTTLED FRUITS, OR FRUITS PRESERVED
WITHOUT SUGAR.

CHOOSE wide-mouthed bottles, which are made for this purpose,
let them be clean and perfectly dry ; gather the fruit during dry
weather, and fill the bottles if possible on the same day; shake the
fruit well down by knocking the bottom edge of the bottle on the
table ; prepare some corks or bungs (which are made for fruit bottles
by being cut the contrary way of the grain); pour boiling water over
them, which will deprive them of any smell or dirt; repeat this a
second time, if necessary, letting them remain in the water each
time until it is cold ; cork the bottles well, and tie them over with
wire or string. M. Appert recommends that they should be luted
with a mixture made of fresh slaked lime and soft cheese ; this is to
be spread on rags and tied over the mouth of the bottle; they are
then placed in a boiler and cold water as far as their mouths ; a cover
is put on with a piece of linen round it to prevent evaporation, the
water is then heated to boiling, and is kept at this point until it is
considered that the fruit is boiled in their own water or juice ; the
fire is then withdrawn, and they are suffered to remain in the water
for an hour, when it may be drawn off. The method which I in
general pursue is to raise the water to the boiling point, and keep it at
this heat for about an hour, according to the nature of the fruit; they
are then suffered to remain in the water until it is cold. I find this
way generally successful. When they are taken out, cover the
mouth of the bottle with melted rosin or bottle wax.

This method is much superior to that of preparing them with water,
which renders the fruit flat, dead, and insipid, the whole of the flavour of the fruit being imparted to the water, except when bottled
very green, when it does not lose it so much.

A method I have tried with pretty good success, is to obtain the
fruit before it is ripe, bottle it, and fill the bottles with cold spring
water, in which are dissolved some oxymuriate of potass, cork them
close, and cover the mouths with rosin. Plums done in this way had
the natural bloom on them. I found these were better than those
done in a similar manner by heat. A few bottles of them fermented.
After the fermentation was over I corked them close, and in six
months I opened some, when they had a smell like wine, and were
not so flat as those which were well preserved by heat, and filled
with water ; these certainly look well to the eye, but they are only
fit to be used for large pies, when the water should be made into a
syrup with sugar, and put in with it.

The first method, which is the same as Appert's, or nearly so, is
decidedly the best; it retains the natural flavour, and may be used
for any purpose it is required, it being as good as fresh fruit.

The pulp or juice of fruits may also be preserved in the same way; if the fruit is not ripe enough to pulp, put it into a jar, and stop it close, place it in a kettle of cold water, heat it until it boils, and let it continue at this point for ten minutes or a quarter of an hour; take it out and pass the pulp through a hair-sieve; bottle, and finish as before.

This method of M. Appert's is not altogether original, but was anticipated by the experiments of Mr. Boyle. A system somewhat on the same principle has been practised by many in the trade for years, which is this. The fruit is bottled and carefully corked, the bottles are then placed on the top of the oven, where they are suffered to remain for twenty-four or forty-eight hours, according to the temperature, which is generally from 120° to 140° Fahrenheit's thermometer. At one place I ascertained the heat during the process, and it averaged 130°. Another system practised is that of heating the bottles in a cool oven.

The principle endeavoured to be accomplished is to destroy the small portion of oxygen contained in the bottle after being corked, by converting it into carbonic acid gas; but some other unknown agent must be produced, as this may be done without heat, which the fermentation of the fruit would cause by itself; for, according to the experiments of Hildebrand, had the oxygen of the atmosphere remained unaltered, it would have caused putrefaction; for he found that oxygen mixed with a small quantity of azote, promoted putrefaction more than pure oxygen. He found that hydrogen gas was the greatest preservative, nitrous next, and after this carbonic. These experiments were tried on meat, but they may be equally applicable in respect to fruit, when the auxiliary produced by heat is not definitely known.

Fruit should always be bottled and boiled on the same day it is gathered; for the longer the fruit lies together the more it sweats; fermentation commences, which is accelerated in the bottles by heat, and there is great danger of their bursting.

All decayed or bruised fruit should be carefully excluded, and that should be preferred which is not quite ripe.

When finished, the bottle should be kept in a cool dry place.

SECTION XVII.—OF COOLING DRINKS FOR BALLS AND ROUTS.

THESE may be made either with fresh fruit, jam, or syrups. The last merely requires the addition of water and lemon-juice to make them palatable.

Gooseberry, Currant, Raspberry, and Strawberry Waters. — Mash either of these fruits when ripe, and press out the juice through a hair-sieve, add a little water to it, and give it a boil; then filter it through a flannel bag, some syrup, a little lemon-juice and water, to make it palatable, but rich, although not too sweet, which is often the fault with these and compotes; ice them the same as wine, and serve.

Cherry Water.—Pound the cherries with the stones to obtain the flavour of the kernel, and make as above.

Apricot and Peach Water as cherry water: or, if made from jam, add a few bitter almonds pounded quite fine, using a little water and lemon-juice to pound them with; add them to the jam with water and lemon-juice to palate; strain it through a lawn sieve, ice, and serve.

Ôrgeat Water.—Blanch half a pound of sweet almonds and one ounce of bitter; pound them very fine in a mortar, using water to prevent their oiling; use one quart of water and a glass of orange-flower water, and make as directed for orgeat syrup; add sugar to palate, strain it through a lawn sieve, ice, and serve.

Lemonade.—Rub off the yellow rinds of six lemons on sugar; squeeze out their juice, and add to it a pint and a half of water, and half a pint of syrup, the white of an egg, with the sugar which has imbibed the oil from the rind; mix them well together; if not to your palate, alter it; strain through a flannel bag, ice, and serve.

Orangeade is made as lemonade, using China oranges instead of the lemons.

SECTION XVIII.—ICES.

[THERE is no article of the dessert kind that deserves a more elevated position than well-made ices, as well for their intrinsic merit as for the agreeable *goût* which they impart to a well-got-up entertainment.

Philadelphia has for a long time enjoyed a pre-eminent reputation in the manufacture of these delicious compounds; the rage however for *cheap* articles, without a due regard to their merits, has made sad inroads into the business; and, in order to accommodate this spirit of retrenchment, ignorant pretenders have consented to the base practice of making inferior articles, which they palm off on the unwary under the specious guise of economy. With these persons it is a custom to use three-fourths milk and only one-fourth of the legitimate article, cream, and, in order to procure a sufficient body, to intermix boiled flour, arrowroot, or potatoe flour; also to flavour with tartaric acid instead of fresh lemons, tonquin bean instead of vanilla, and inferior fruits when the best only should be used.

We mention these facts in order to caution young beginners against any such fatal mistakes. The best ingredients should *always* be used. Obtain your cream invariably fresh from a dairyman who is tenacious of his reputation, and who is known to produce a pure rich article; *it cannot be too good,* and if not used immediately should be kept in ice until wanted. Good cream cannot be had (even where large quantities are used) for a less price than twenty cents per quart. Use cream entirely, and on no account mingle the slightest quantity of milk, which detracts materially from the richness and smoothness of the ices. Always use the finest flavoured to be obtained, and follow implicitly the following very copious directions, and you will be certain to be rewarded by a fine article, of which you may well be proud :]

Utensils requisite for making.—1st. Pewter pots of various sizes, suitable to the quantity of mixture intended to be frozen. Tin or zinc will not answer the purpose, as it congeals the mixture too quickly without allowing it a sufficient time to become properly incorporated, and forms it in lumps like hailstones.

2d. Half pint, pint, pint and a half, and quart moulds, and some in the form of fruits made to open in the centre with a hinge : these also require to be made of the same material.

3d. Ice pails. These should be adapted to the size of the pots, about the same depth, and eight or ten inches more in diameter; if even greater, it is immaterial, the depth being the principal consideration, for the deeper it is the greater caution is required to prevent the salt from entering the mixture; for as the ice dissolves, the pot descends, and the water runs under the cover, which, being salt, spoils the contents; neither have you a sufficient basis whereon the pot rests so as to mix your creams, &c., with the spatula; consequently, half your exertions are lost by its constant sinking when you apply the least effort to scrape it from the sides. There should be a hole near the bottom, with a cork fitted into it, so as to be drawn at pleasure, that the water may be allowed to run off when there is too much.

4th. The spatula. This is an instrument somewhat resembling a gardener's spade; it should be made of stout copper and tinned, the blade being about four inches long by three in width, round at the end, and having a socket to receive a wooden handle; this is for scraping the cream, &c., from the sides of the pot as it freezes, and for mixing it.

5th. Either a large mortar and pestle, or a strong box and mallet for pounding the ice.

6th. A spade wherewith to mix the ice and salt together, fixing your pails, &c.

7th. A tin case or box, with a kind of drawer fitted to it so as to be drawn out at pleasure, and having shelves or divisions; this is for keeping the ices in the form of fruits, after they are finished, until required for the table.

To freeze Ices.—This is accomplished through the medium of ice. Of itself it does not contain sufficient frigorific power to congeal a liquid body to the required consistence without an auxiliary; the usual one employed is that of salt. As a general rule, take about two pounds to every six pounds of ice, which I think will be nearly the quantity required. I cannot state precisely, as it is the custom to mix it by guess; but note, the freezing quality depends on the quantity of salt which is used, consequently, the more there is mixed with the ice the quicker are the creams, &c., frozen.

Pound a sufficient quantity of ice small, and let some salt be well mixed with it; place the pot containing the mixture in a pail, which you fill (the latter) with pounded ice and salt as far as the lid; strew a handful of salt on the top of the ice, let it remain a few minutes until you have similarly disposed of others, as three or four may be done at a time if required, then whirl them round briskly by means of the handles for five minutes, take off the lids one at a time, and with the spatula stir or carry the unfrozen part well round the sides, turning the pot also with the left hand; continue this for two or three minutes, which serves to soften what has already frozen, as well as helps to freeze the remaining portion; then scrape it from the sides, put on the lids, whirl round again briskly, as before directed, repeating the same operations every four or five minutes. As it forms into consistence, do not spare your labour in well working or mixing it together when you scrape it down, so as to make it perfectly smooth and free from lumps, for the smoothness of your ice depends on this operation; continue to freeze until the whole is well set. Ice when well frozen should be about the consistence of butter, tough to the reel, of a good colour, and without any lumps in it. Those which contain too much syrup cannot be frozen to the degree required, and those which have too little freeze hard, and feel short and crisp, like compressed or frozen snow, which arises from having too many watery particles in it, by the excess of either water or milk according to the nature of your ice. In either case it may be ascertained when you commence freezing, by the first coat which is formed round the sides. It should then be altered by either adding more cream or water, with juice, or pulp of fruit, or other flavouring matter in proportion, as the case may be, if too rich, and *vice versâ*, by the addition of more syrup, &c., when poor; but at all times the necessity of altering them should be avoided, as the component parts cannot be so perfectly blended together, without considerable extra labour, as if they were properly mixed at the commencement.

During the time of freezing, or after the creams, &c., are moulded and set up, if there is too much water in the pail, the frigorific power is lessened; a little increases it, as at first it is only a solution of the salt; but as the ice dissolves and mixes with it, it decreases; therefore, when it comes to the top drain it off, and fill up with fresh salt and ice.

When the ices are properly frozen, take out the pots, drain off the water, empty the pail, again replace them and fill them with fresh salt and ice, as before; then spread the creams over the sides of the pot, when they are ready for use, if they are intended to be served in a shop or by glassfulls. Should it be required for moulds, line the bottom with a piece of paper, before you put it on; if there is no impression or figure on the top, you may cover that also with paper; in filling them press it well in, so as to fill every part; leave a little projecting above the surface to form the top, which you put on ; pack the moulds in a pail, and fill the vacancies with pounded ice well mixed with plenty of salt, strew a handful also on the top.

Ices should be moulded from half an hour to an hour before they are required to be served.

When you want to turn them out, wash the mould well in cold water that no salt may remain on it ; take off the bottom and top, and the ice will come out easily.

For fruit moulds, fill each with either cream or water ice of the same kind as that which you would represent, and for the better resemblance to nature, preserve the stone with the stalk and leaves of each, which put in their proper places, allowing the leaves to project outside ; close the mould, wrap it in paper, and place it in ice as others ; when you want to turn them out, wash the shape in lukewarm water to take off the paper, and be careful that you do not injure the leaves, as they will often be found frozen to it ; dip it again in water, open it and take out the ice, which you colour to nature with camel's-hair pencils and liquid colour (see Colours); the down or bloom is represented by dusting it with dry colour in powder, tied in a small thin muslin bag, or by means of a dry camel's-hair pencil ; line the shelves of the case with paper or vine leaves, and put in the fruit as it is finished ; let the case be surrounded with pounded ice and salt, as for moulds.

Ices may be divided into three classes, viz : cream, custard, and water. These derive their names from the basis of which they are composed, the flavouring matter mixed with it giving the other defi nition ; thus we say, raspberry cream and raspberry water ; but custard ices are not so particularly defined as the others by the basis, and either only receives the name of the flavour given to it, or as that of cream.

Cream Ices. — These are composed entirely of pure fresh cream, with the juice or pulp of fruit either fresh or preserved, and syrup or sugar so blended together as the taste of one may not predominate over that of another ; but if either is in excess it should be that of the fruit.

Raspberry of fresh fruit. — One quart of raspberries, one quart of cream, three-quarters of a pound or a pound of sugar, a few ripe currants and gooseberries, or currants and ripe cherries may be added, instead of all raspberries, which is much approved by some, and the juice of two lemons ; * mash the fruit, and pass it through a sieve to take out the skins and seeds ; mix it with the other articles ; add a little prepared cochineal to heighten the colour ; put it in the pot and freeze.

---

* The quantity of fruit required for these ices will depend, in a great measure, on the quality of the fruit and the seasons in which it is produced ; a pint and a half will be found sufficient when it is good in fine seasons ; the quantity stated in each weight is the greatest required.

Note.—All ices made with red fruit require this addition of cochineal.

Raspberry, from Jam. — One pound of jam, one quart of cream, about six ounces of sugar or syrup, to palate, and the juice of two lemons. Mix as before.

Strawberry.—As raspberry.

Currant Ice from fresh Fruit.—One pint and a half of ripe currants, half a pint of raspberries, one quart of cream, the juice of two lemons, and twelve ounces of sugar. Mix as raspberry.

Currant Ice.—Preserved Fruit.—The same proportions as raspberry, using either jam or jelly.

Barberry Ice.—Use the same proportions as before. For fresh barberries, first soften them by either boiling them in the syrup you intend to use, or put them in a stew-pan, and stir them over the fire until tender; pass them through a sieve, mix, and freeze as raspberry. The barberries, having much acid, do not require any lemon-juice to be mixed with them.

Apricot.—Fresh Fruit.—Twenty-four fine ripe apricots, one quart of cream, twelve ounces of sugar, the juice of two lemons, with a few of the kernels blanched; mash the apricots, rub them through a sieve, mix, and freeze.

Apricot, from Jam.—Twelve ounces of jam, one quart of cream, the juice of two lemons, eight ounces of sugar, a few kernels or bitter almonds blanched and pounded fine; rub the whole through a sieve, and freeze.

Peach Ice.—The same proportions as apricot.

Pine Apple—Fresh Fruit.—One pound of fresh pine apple, half a pint of syrup in which a pine has been preserved, two or three slices of pine apple cut in small dice, and the juice of three lemons; pound or grate the apple, pass it through a sieve, mix, and freeze.

Pine Apple—Preserved Fruit.—Eight ounces of preserved pine, four slices cut in small dice, one quart of cream, the juice of three lemons, and sufficient syrup from the pine to sweeten it; pound the preserved pine, mix lemons with the cream, &c., and freeze.

Ginger Ice.—Six ounces of preserved ginger, one quart of cream, half a pint of the syrup from the ginger, sugar sufficient to sweeten it with, and the juice of two lemons; pound the ginger in a mortar, add the cream, &c., and freeze.

[*Brahma Ice.*—One quart of cream, the whites of ten eggs, one and a half pounds of powdered sugar of the best quality; mix the whole in a tin saucepan; put it on the fire, stirring constantly, until it boils once, then add two wine-glasses of Curaçoa, half a glass of orange-flower water; put it into the pot, and freeze.]

Orange Ice Cream.—Six oranges, three lemons, one quart of cream, and twelve ounces of sugar or of syrup, to palate; rub off the yellow rind of two or three of the oranges on part of the sugar, scrape it off with a knife, squeeze out the juice of the oranges and lemons, and strain it; mix it with the cream and the sugar on which the rind was rubbed, add the other part of the sugar, dissolve and freeze.

China Orange Ice Cream.—Eight oranges, two lemons, one quart of cream, twelve ounces of sugar ; rub off the rind of four or five of the oranges and one lemon on sugar, squeeze, and strain the juice ; add the cream, &c., mix, and freeze.

Cherry Ice Cream.—Two pounds of cherries, one quart of cream, and twelve ounces of sugar or syrup; pound the cherries, with the stones, in a mortar, adding a few ripe gooseberries or currants if approved of; pass the pulp through a sieve, add the cream and sugar with the juice of two lemons and a little cochineal, mix, and freeze.

With preserved fruit it is made the same way, adding a little noyau, or a few bitter almonds pounded for the flavour of the kernel.

[*Harlequin Ice.*—This is formed by putting a small quantity of each kind of ice into the same mould, taking care to have as great a variety of colours as possible placed so as to produce a contrast; cover the mould with salt and ice as before directed, and let it remain half an hour, when it will be fit to turn out. When the colours are tastily disposed of, it produces a good effect for the table, but is not much admired on account of the jumble of flavours.]

Lemon Ice Cream.—Six large lemons, one quart of cream, and twelve ounces of sugar or half pint of syrup; grate off the peels of three of the lemons into a basin, squeeze the juice to it, let it stand for two or three hours, strain, add the cream and syrup, and freeze or mix as Seville orange ice.

Mille Fruit Cream Ice.—Make a lemon cream ice, and flavour it with elder flowers, mix in some preserved dried fruits and peels cut in small pieces.   Before it is moulded, sprinkle it with prepared cochineal, and mix it a little, so as it may appear in veins or marbled.

Custard Ices.—These are similarly composed to the cream ices, with the addition of six eggs to each quart of cream.   All kinds of nuts, liqueurs, essences, infusions, or biscuits, are principally mixed with it.

Custard for Ices.—One quart of cream, six eggs, and twelve ounces of powdered loaf sugar; break the eggs into a stew-pan, and whisk them together ; add the cream and sugar ; when well mixed, place it on the fire, and continue stirring it from the bottom with the whisk, to prevent burning; until it gets thick; take it from the fire, continue to stir it for a few minutes, and pass it through a sieve.   If the custard be suffered to boil, it will curdle.

Plombiere Ice, or Swiss Pudding.—Take one pint and a half of cream and half a pint of milk, and make them into a custard with seven yolks of eggs; flavour it either with Curaçoa, Maraschino, or rum, freeze the custard, and add about a quarter of a pound of dried cherries, orange, lemon, and citron peel, and currants; mix these in the iced custard. The Curaçoa, or rum, &c., may be poured over the fruit when you commence freezing, or before, which I consider preferable to flavouring the custard. Prepare the mould, which is round, and something in the shape of a melon, made to open in the centre with a hinge. Strew over the inside with some clean currants, fill the mould, and close it; immerse it in some fresh ice mixed with salt. Before it is required to be turned out, prepare a dish as follows:—

The Sauce.—Make a little custard, and flavour it with brandy; dissolve some isinglass in water or milk, and when it is nearly cold add sufficient to the custard to set it; pour it into the dish you intend to serve it on. As soon as it is set, turn out the pudding on it and serve.

Almond or Orgeat Ice Cream.—One quart of cream, eight ounces of sweet almonds, two ounces of bitter almonds, twelve ounces of sugar, and two ounces of orange-flower water; blanch the almonds, and pound them quite fine in a mortar, using the orange-flower water in pounding, to prevent their oiling: rub them through a sieve, and pound again the remaining portion which has not passed through, until they are fine enough; then mix them with the cream, and make it into a custard with eggs, as the preceding; strain, and when cold, freeze.

Pistachio Ice Cream.—One quart of cream, eight ounces of pistachios, and twelve ounces of sugar; blanch and pound the pistachios with a little of the cream; mix and finish as orgeat ice, flavouring it with a little essence of cédrat, or the rind of a fresh citron rubbed on sugar; or the custard may be flavoured by boiling in it a little cinnamon and mace and the rind of of a lemon.

Filbert Ice Cream.—One quart of cream, one pound of nuts, and twelve ounces of sugar or one pint of syrup; break the nuts, and roast the kernels in the oven; when done, pound them with a little cream, make a custard, and finish as almond ice.

Chestnut Ice.—As the preceding, taking off the husks and skin.

Burnt Filbert Ice Cream.—Use the same proportions as in filbert ice; put the kernels into the syrup, and boil till it comes to the blow; stir the sugar with a spatula, that it may grain and adhere to the nuts; when cold, pound them with the sugar quite fine; make a custard, and mix them with it, allowing for the sugar that is used for the nuts; mix, and freeze as the others.

Burnt Almond Ice Cream.—Make as burnt filbert ice.

Coffee Ice Cream.—One quart of cream, five ounces of Mocha coffee, and twelve ounces of sugar; roast the coffee in a coarse iron or other stew-pan, keeping it constantly stirred until it is a good brown colour throw it into the custard cream whilst it is quite hot, and cover it closely; let it infuse for an hour or two, then strain and freeze.

The cream may be made with an infusion of coffee, thus: take the quantity of coffee, fresh roasted and ground to a fine powder; put this into a common glass bottle or decanter, and pour on it sufficient cold river water to moisten the powder and make an infusion; stop the bottle close, and let it remain all night; the next day filter the infusion by passing it through some fine lawn or blotting paper placed in a glass funnel; by this process a very strong and superior infusion is obtained, which contains the whole of the aroma of the coffee. Dr. Ratier observes, — "I have tried this process with boiling and with cold water; and I have assured myself, by comparison, that the powder drained by the cold water, and treated then with boiling water, gave nothing but a water slightly tinted with yellow, and devoid of odour and flavour. It is, besides, proper to pass an equal quantity of water to the first, over the grounds, in order that the second water may serve for new powder." Use this for flavouring the custard, and freeze.

Chocolate Ice. — One quart of cream, six ounces of chocolate, and ten ounces of sugar; dissolve the chocolate in a little water, or make the sugar into a syrup, and dissolve it by putting it on the side of the stove, or over the fire; add the cream and eggs, and make it into a custard as before; when cold, freeze.

Tea Ice.—One quart of cream, two ounces of the best green tea, and twelve ounces of sugar; put the tea into a cup, and pour on it a little cold river water in which has been dissolved a small portion of carbonate of soda, about as much as may be placed on a fourpenny piece; let it remain for an hour or two, then add a little boiling water, sufficient in the whole to make a very strong infusion; or the boiling water may be dispensed with, adding more cold water in proportion, and letting it soak longer, when a superior infusion will be obtained; strain it, and add to the cream and eggs. Finish as the others.

Vanilla Ice.—One quart of cream, half an ounce of vanilla, twelve ounces of sugar; cut the vanilla into small pieces, and pound it with the sugar until it is quite fine, add it to the cream and eggs, make it into a custard, strain, and when cold freeze, or it may be flavoured with the essence of vanilla. (See Essences).

Noyau Cream Ice. — Make a custard cream, and flavour it with noyau; finish as almond ice.

Maraschino Cream Ice.—Make as noyau, flavouring it with Maraschino de Zara. All liqueur ices are made the same way, using the different liqueurs with which each is named, or they may be made in this way :—Take a quart of cream, put it into the ice-pot with six ounces of sugar, which you place in the ice; work or whisk it well about the sides with a whisk for five minutes; add a glassful of liqueur, work this well together, then whisk the whites of two eggs to a strong froth, add two ounces of sugar to them, mix this well with the cream, and freeze to the required consistence. This produces a very beautiful, soft, and mellow cream.

Water Ices. — These are the pulp or juice of fruits mixed with syrup, lemon juice, and a little water, so as to bring them to a good flavour and consistence when frozen.

Currant Water Ice.—Two pounds of ripe currants, eight ounces of raspberries and ripe cherries, one pint of syrup, and one pint of water.

Pick and mash the fruit, and strain it through a sieve, add the syrup and water, put it in the ice-pot and freeze.

Cherry Water Ice. — Cherries two pounds, either Kentish or May Duke, ripe gooseberries four ounces, one pint of syrup, half a pint of water, and the juice of two lemons; pound the cherries with the stones in a mortar, pass the juice of the fruit through a sieve, mix the syrup and water with it, and freeze; if it should not freeze sufficiently, add a little more water.

Gooseberry Water Ice.—Ripe gooseberries two pounds, the red hairy sort is the best, one pound of cherries, one pint of syrup, one pint of water, and the juice of two lemons; mash the fruit and pass it through a sieve, mix it with the syrup and water, and freeze.

Raspberry Water Ice.—One quart of ripe raspberries, four ounces of ripe cherries and currants, half a pint of syrup, half a pint of water, and the juice of two lemons. Mash the fruit and pass the juice through a sieve, mix the syrup water and lemon with it, and freeze.

Raspberry Water Ice. — Two pottles of the best scarlet pines, one pint of syrup, half a pint of water, and the juice of two lemons.

Mix as currant. All red fruits require the addition of a little prepared cochineal to heighten the colour.

Apricot Water Ice.—Eighteen or twenty fine ripe apricots, according to their size, half a pint of syrup, half a pint of water, the juice of two lemons.

Mash the apricots and pass them through a sieve, mix the pulp with the syrup water and lemon-juice, break the stones, blanch the kernels, and pound them fine with a little water, pass them through a sieve, add it to the mixture, and freeze.

Peach Water Ice.—One pound of the pulp of ripe peaches, half a pint of syrup, half a pint of water, the juice of two lemons. Mix as apricot. If the fruit is not ripe enough to pulp, open them and take out the stones, put them in a stew-pan with the syrup and water, boil until tender, and pass them through a sieve; mix in the pounded kernels; when cold, freeze.

Damson Ice.—One quart of damsons, one pint of syrup, half a pint of water. Mix as peach ice. Magnum-bonums, Orleans, green gages, or any other plum may be done in the same way.

Pine-apple Water Ice.—Half a pint of pine syrup, one pint of water, the juice of two lemons, and three or four slices of preserved pine cut into small dice; mix and freeze.

Fresh Pine-apple Water Ice. — One pound of pine-apple, one pint of syrup, half a pint of water, and the juice of two lemons. Cut the pine in pieces, and put it into a stew-pan with the syrup and water, and boil until tender ; pass it through a sieve, add the lemon-juice, with two or three slices of the pine cut in small dice, mix and freeze when cold. The pine may be pounded instead of being boiled, an mixed with the syrup, &c.

The whole of these ices may be made with preserved fruit instead of fresh.

One pound of jam or jelly, one pint of water, the juice of two lem- ons, and syrup sufficient to make it palatable.

Apple-Water Ice. — Pare and core some fine apples, cut them in pieces into a preserving pan with sufficient water for them to float, boil until they are reduced to a marmalade, then strain: to a pint of apple-water add half a pint of syrup, the juice of a lemon, and a little water; when cold, freeze.

Pear-Water Ice.—Prepare as apple ice.

Orange-Water Ice.—One pint of China orange-juice, one pint of syrup, half a pint of water, the juice of four large lemons.

Rub off the yellow rind of six oranges and two lemons on sugar, scrape it off and mix with the strained juice, syrup and water.

Lemon-Water Ice.—Half a pint of lemon juice, half a pint of water, one pint of syrup, the peels of six lemons rubbed off on sugar, or the yellow rind may be pared or grated off, and the juice squeezed to it in a basin; let it remain for an hour or two, then strain, mix, and freeze ; whip up the whites of three eggs to a strong froth, with a little sugar, as for meringues; when the ice is beginning to set, work this well in it, which will make it eat beautifully soft and delicious; freeze to the required consistence ; if the ice is to be served in glasses, the meringue may be added after it has been frozen. Orange-water ice may be done the same.

Maraschino-Water Ice.—Make a lemon ice as the above, using less water, and making up the deficiency with Maraschino; but be careful the taste of the lemon does not prevail too much; add more water and syrup to correct it if it does. Noyau and all other liqueur ices are made the same way, using that to flavour the lemon ice which it bears the name of. Champagne and wine ices the same.

Punch-Water Ice. — Make either a good lemon ice, or use some orange-juice with the lemons, in the proportion of one orange to two lemons; either rub off the yellow rind of the lemons on sugar, or pare it very thin, and soak it in the spirit for a few hours; when the ice is beginning to set, work in the whites of three eggs to each quart, beaten to a strong froth, and mixed with sugar as for meringue, or add the whites without whisking them; when it is nearly frozen, take out the pot from the ice, and mix well with it a glass each of rum and brandy, or sufficient to make it a good flavour; some like the taste of the rum to predominate, but in this case of course you will be guided by the wish of your employer. In general the prevailing flavour distinguishes it by name, as rum-punch or brandy-punch ice; after the spirit is well mixed, replace the pot and finish freezing. If champagne, arrack, or tea is added, it is then termed champagne-punch ice, arrack-punch ice, &c.

Punch à la Romaine—Roman Punch Ice.—Make a quart of lemon ice, and flavour it with a glass or two of each, of rum, brandy, champagne, and Maraschino; when it is frozen, to each quart take the whites of five eggs and whip them to a very strong froth; boil half a pound of sugar to the ball, and rub it with a spoon or spatula against the sides to grain it; when it turns white, mix it quickly with the whites of eggs, stir it lightly together, and add it to the ice; when cold, mix it well together, and serve it in glasses; less sugar must be used in the ice, so as to allow for that which is used in making the meringue.

Mille Fruit Water Ice.—Make a good lemon ice, with a pint of syrup, half a pint of water, and as much strained lemon-juice as will give it the desired flavour, with some elder flowers infused in syrup; when the ice is frozen, mix it in some preserved green fruits and peels cut in small dice; if any large fruits are used, such as apricots, peaches, pine-apples, &c., they must be also cut in dice like the peels; sprinkle it with prepared cochineal, and mix it a little so as it may appear in veins.

SECTION XIX.—JELLIES.

[*Calves' Feet Jellies.*—Boil down one set of calves' feet in four quarts of water till it is reduced to one half, then strain through a sieve, in order to remove the bones; when settled and cold take off the grease on the surface, then boil, with the following additions:—twelve eggs, three pints of good Madeira wine, and two pounds of loaf sugar, the juice of four lemons; stir the mixture well with a whisk or spatula, and filter through a fine flannel bag. Jellies of Champagne and other wines are made in the same manner.

Coffee Jelly is made the same as preceding, using, instead of Madeira wine, a decoction of coffee, prepared as follows:—infuse half a pound of roasted Mocha coffee, pulverised or ground, in one quart of water, strain off the decoction, and add to it a little brandy.

Tea Jelly—Green or Black.—Treat in the same way, using an infusion of half an ounce of tea to one quart of water.

FRUIT JELLIES.

Strawberry Jelly.—One pound of picked strawberries, press them lightly, and put them in four ounces of clear syrup; cover the infusion, and let them stand all night; strain through a bag on the following morning: in the mean time clarify half a pound of sugar; when nearly clarified add to it a few drops of prepared cochineal, to give it a fine red colour; after which, strain it through a sieve, and add to it an ounce of clarified isinglass, the juice of two sound lemons, and afterwards the fruit; stir the jelly gently, and put it in a mould placed in ice.

N. B.—To clarify isinglass, take one ounce of the best Russia cut it in small pieces, wash it several times in clear warm water, put it on the fire in a small pan with one pint of soft water, let it boil sufficiently, taking care to skim it well; when it is reduced to one-half, strain through a napkin into a clean vessel. The sugar and isinglass should be only lukewarm when you mix them. These remarks apply to all jellies of this kind.

Pine Apple Jelly.—Take a fine ripe pine apple, cut it small, and strain the juice through a hair sieve, then throw it into the boiling syrup, let it boil up, and when nearly cold strain it through a silk sieve, add a little caramel to give the jelly a fine yellow tinge; then the juice of two fine lemons, and an ounce of clarified isinglass. Proceed as before.

Jelly of Apricots.—Take the stones out of one dozen and a half of fine ripe apricots and boil them in the syrup, which, in this case, should be as light coloured as possible; when boiled sufficiently to extract the flavour, strain through a napkin, add the necessary quantity of isinglass, and finish as usual.

Orange Jelly.—Squeeze the juice out of twelve Havanna oranges and one lemon, strain through a fine linen cloth, then mix with the syrup boiled to the ball; add the clarified isinglass, filter through a fine flannel bag, and finish as before.

The foregoing will suffice for all fruit jellies.

BLANC MANGE.

Take four ounces of sweet almonds blanched, half an ounce of bitter almonds, pound them in a clean mortar, moisten them gradually with orange-flower water, mix this with one quart of fresh cream and one ounce of clarified isinglass, put into a saucepan, constantly stirring till it boils, then pass through a fine sieve, and form into a mould, and put on ice.

Blanc Mange may be flavoured with vanilla, Mocha coffee, marischino, pistachios, and strawberries; in which case the bitter almonds should be left out.]

SECTION XX.—ON ESSENCES.

THE essences or essential oils sold for general use are or ought to be obtained by distillation; but for many purposes they may be obtained equally as good, and, in some cases, superior, without. As these are often adulterated with olive or nut oils, or with spirits of wine, the fixed oils may be detected by pouring some of the suspected essence on a piece of clean writing paper, and holding it before the fire; the quantity of fixed oil it contains will remain, leaving a greasy mark, whereas the pure essential oil will evaporate without leaving any appearance; if spirits of wine be added, pour a little water or oil of turpentine into the adulterated sample, and it will turn milky, as the two will not unite without producing this effect. It is often sophisticated with the oil of turpentine, which is the lightest of all essential oils; in this case, rub a drop over the hand and hold it by the fire, when it may be recognized by the smell, or if burnt it will give out a dense black smoke.

Rectified spirits of wine dissolve the volatile oil and resin of vegetables (their taste and smell most frequently reside in these), whilst water acts on the saline and mucilaginous parts. Proof spirit, which is a mixture of both these, extracts all their virtues, and through this we are enabled to obtain the essence or tincture of any vegetable, of superior quality to that generally sold, and at considerably less expense. The essential oil of lemons or oranges is obtained by rubbing off the yellow rind on the rough surface of a piece of loaf sugar, which is much superior for flavour to that produced by any other means. Scrape off the sugar after it has imbibed the oil, and dry it in a gentle heat, put it into small glazed pots, and tie them over with bladder; it will keep any length of time unimpaired. The same observation holds good as regards all fruit whose flavour or essential oil resides in its peel.

Essence of Lemon.—Eight ounces of lemon peel, ten ounces of rectified spirits of wine. Pare or grate off the yellow rind of the lemon very thin and weigh it, put it into a bottle and pour the spirit on it, stop it close, and let it steep for fourteen days, when it is fit for use. Proof gin or white rum will serve equally well, but not such as is generally sold at the gin-shops; this is excellent for ices, creams, lemonade, &c. In many establishments, where quantities of peel are thrown away, the cost of this would be comparatively trifling, compared with the price of the inferior oil generally sold.

Essence of Orange.—Make as lemon, using only four ounces of the yellow rind.

Essence of Bergamot.—From the peel of the bergamot lemon.

Essence de Cédrat.—From the yellow part of the fresh citron peel; it may also be obtained by pressing the yellow part of the peel between two glass plates, and by the distillation of the flowers of the citron-tree.

18

Allspice, Cloves, Cinnamon, or Nutmegs, &c.—Two ounces of spice, one pint of proof spirit. Bruise the spice, put it into a bottle, stop it close, let it remain fourteen days, and filter for use.

The oil from nutmegs is often extracted from them by decoction, before they are brought to the market, and their orifices closed again with powdered sassafras; this may be ascertained by the lightness of the nut; if it is punctured with a pin, the oil will be pressed from it when good. These oils may be obtained by expression or distillation; they hold resin in solution, and consequently sink in water. The essences usually sold are made by adding half an ounce of the pure oil to one pint of spirits of wine.

Essence of Ginger.—The best Jamaica or China ginger two ounces, proof spirit one pint. Powder the ginger, mix it with the spirit, stop close, and let it steep for twelve or fourteen days.

This is the same as is sold for "Oxley's concentrated essence of Jamaica ginger,"—a mere solution of ginger in rectified spirit—*Paris's Pharmacologia.*

Essence of Peppermint.—"A spirituous solution of the essential oil, coloured green by spinach leaves." *Ibid.* This essential oil is obtained by distillation. Four pounds of dried leaves yield one ounce.

Essence of Vanilla.—Vanilla two ounces, water ten ounces, rectified spirit three-quarters of an ounce. Cut the vanilla in small pieces, and pound it fine in a marble mortar, with loaf sugar (about a pound), adding the white of an egg and the spirit. Put it into a glazed pot, tie a piece of writing paper over it, and make a hole in it with a pin; stand the pot in warm water, keeping it at that heat for twenty-four hours, then strain for use.

One drachm of this is equal to an ounce of vanilla, and is excellent for flavouring ices, creams, liqueurs, &c.

Essence of Bitter Almonds.—This is obtained by distilling the cake or residue of the almonds after the oil has been expressed from them. It is a deadly poison, containing prussic acid, like all other nuts or leaves, which possess the bitter principle. Flies drop dead when passing over the still when it is in operation. The essence usually sold is one ounce of oil to seven ounces of rectified spirit.

SECTION XXI.—MERINGUES AND ICING.

Dry Meringues in the form of Eggs.—Ten whites of eggs, twelve ounces of sugar.

Obtain the newest laid eggs, and separate the white from the yolk very carefully; put the whites into a pan, which must be quite free from grease; whisk them to a very strong froth, so as it will support an egg, or even a greater weight; have the sugar pounded and sifted through a lawn sieve, and mix it as lightly as possible; spread some pieces of board about an inch thick, then with a table or dessert spoon drop them on the paper about two inches asunder, dust them with fine powdered loaf sugar, blow off all that does not adhere, and put them into a cool oven to bake until they are a nice light brown; if the oven should be too warm, when the surface gets dry or hardened cover them with paper; as soon as they are done take them off with a knife, press the inside or soft part down with the top or the back of a spoon, place them on sieves, and put them into the stove to dry; when they are required to be served fill them with any kind of preserved fruit or cream, if it is rather acid the better, and put two together.

The quality of the meringues will depend on the eggs being well whipped to a very strong froth, and also on the quantity of sugar, for if there is not enough they will eat tough.

[*Kisses.*—Twelve ounces of sugar powdered very fine and passed through a silk sieve, the whites of six eggs beaten to a strong froth; mix and lay out on paper, as for dry meringues: when baked, place two together. The size should be about that of a pigeon's egg.]

Italian Meringues.—One pound of sugar, the whites of six eggs. Clarify the sugar and boil it to the blow; in the mean time whip up the whites as for the last, take the sugar from the fire and rub it a little against the sides of the pan to grain it; as soon as it begins to turn white, mix in the whipped eggs, stirring the sugar well from the bottom and sides of the pan with the whisk or spatula; lay them off, and bake as dry meringues; these may be coloured by adding the liquid colour to the syrup so as to give the desired tint; and either of them may be flavoured by rubbing off the peel of oranges, lemons, or cédrats on sugar, and scraping it off as it imbibes the oil; or it may be flavoured with vanilla, by cutting it in small pieces and pounding it with some sugar, or with any liqueur by adding a spoonful or two when you mix the eggs or sugar. They may also be varied in form, and baked on tin or iron plates instead of wood, that the bottoms may be quite firm. The tops may be covered with almonds or pistachios, blanched and cut small or in fillets, or with currants, or coloured sugars; the whole depending on the taste and ingenuity of the artist.

Mushrooms.—To make these, take either of the pastes for meringues or light icing, as for cakes; put some into a bag in the shape of a cone, with a tin pipe at the end, the same as used for Savoy biscuits; lay them off in drops the size you wish them to be, on iron plates rubbed quite clean and dry, bake them as you would meringues, make also a smaller drop to form the stalk; when they are baked, take them off the tin and scoop out a little with your finger from the bottom near the edge, to form the hollow rough surface underneath; then dry them in the stove; scrape some chocolate and dissolve it in a little warm water, and rub a little over the rough part underneath; then place the stalk in the centre, fixing it with a little icing, and let the flat part which was on the tin be placed outermost to represent where it was cut.

Icing for Wedding or Twelfth Cakes, &c. — Pound, and sift some treble-refined sugar through a lawn sieve, and put it into an earthen pan, which must be quite free from grease; to each pound of sifted sugar add the whites of three eggs, or sufficient to make it into a paste of a moderate consistence, then with a wooden spoon or spatula beat it well, using a little lemon-juice occasionally, and more white of egg if you find that it will bear it without making it too thin, until you have a nice light icing, which will hang to the sides of the pan and spoon; or, if it is dropped from the spoon, it should remain on the top without speedily losing the form it assumed. A pan of icing, when well beat and finished, should contain as much again in bulk as it was at the commencement: use sufficient lemon-juice to give the icing a slight acid, or it will scale off the cake in large pieces when it is cut. Many prefer the pyroligneous acid to the lemon-juice, but the flavour is not so delicate, and it always retains a smell of the acid; neither did I ever find, as some assert, that it improves the quality and appearance of the icing; the only advantage derived from it is that of economy.

On piping Cakes, Bon-bons, &c. — This is a method of ornamenting wedding, twelfth-cakes, and other articles with icing, by means of small pipes or tubes; these are most generally made with writing-paper folded in the form of a cone, in the same manner as a grocer makes up his papers for small lots of sugar, tea, &c. The tube is filled with icing, made as for cakes, the base of the cone, or the place where it was filled, is turned down to prevent the sides opening, and the escape of the icing; the point is then cut off with a sharp knife or scissors, so as to make a hole sufficiently large to form the icing, when squeezed or pressed out, in a thread of the required size, and which will either be fine or coarse according to the length of the point which is cut off. If the hole at the point of the cone is not perfectly straight when the icing is pressed out, it will form a spiral thread, which is very inconvenient to work with. Stars, borders, flowers, and different devices, are formed on cakes after they are iced, the execution of which depends on the ability and ingenuity of the artist. Baskets, Chinese and other temples, &c., are formed on moulds by these means, first giving them a coating of white wax, which is brushed over them after it is melted, and when cold, the icing is formed on it like trellis-work; when finished, the mould is warmed, and the icing easily comes off. Some of the pipes which are used cannot be formed with paper, as the tape and star-pipes, which are made of tin, having a bag fastened to them in a similar manner to that generally used for dropping out Savoy biscuits, macaroons, &c., only much smaller, the point of the tin tube of the one being fluted to form a star, and in the other it is flat, so that when the icing is forced or squeezed through, it comes out in a broad thin sheet, like a piece of tape. I employ a set of pipes made of tin, with small tags fastened to them; these are of different dimensions; the orifice of the round ones commences at the size of a common pin, and the tape pipes from a quarter to half an inch in width. I find these much better than paper ones, as the trouble and time which is lost in constantly making new ones is amply repaid by the others, as they are not very expensive and are always ready for use. These pipes should be in the hands of the confectioner what the pencil or brush is to the painter, —capable of performing wonders with men of genius. Some of the bon-bons, which may be seen in the shops, are proofs of what I assert; and many things are so cleverly done, that many persons would believe that they were either formed in a mould or modelled. I have not space to enlarge further on this subject, but much more might be given in explanation; therefore the artist must be guided by his own genius and fancy.*

SECTION XXII.—GUM PASTE.

TAKE one ounce of picked gum-tragacanth; wash it in water, to take off any dust or dirt; put it into a clean pot, and pour on it rather more than half a pint of water, or sufficient to cover the gum about an inch; stir it frequently, to accelerate the solution; it will take twenty-four hours to dissolve; then squeeze it out through a coarse cloth, as directed for lozenges, taking care that everything employed in the making is very clean, or it will spoil the colour; put it into a mortar. adding gradually six or eight ounces of treble-refined sugar, sifted through a lawn sieve; work it well with the pestle, until it is incorporated and becomes a very white smooth paste; put it into a glazed pot, cover the paste with a damp cloth, and turn the pot upside-down on an even surface, to exclude the air. When it is wanted, take a little of it and put it on a clean marble, and work some more sugar into it (which has been sifted through a lawn sieve) with the fingers, until it is a firm paste, which will break when pulled; if it is not stiff enough, it will roll up under the knife when you cut it from the impressions in your paste-boards; if it is too stiff, work in a little of your prepared paste with it, to soften it. When your paste works harsh and cracks, it has too much gum in it; in this case, use a little water to work it down; and if the gum is too thin it will crack, and dry too soon from the excess of sugar, therefore add some more strained gum that has not been mixed with sugar. The same observation also holds good with respect to lozenges. If it is required coloured, add a little prepared cochineal, or any other colour in fine powder; mix it on the stone. If they are to be flavoured with any essence, add it at the same time. This paste is fit to be eaten, and is the foundation of gum-paste comfits, dragees, &c.

Gum Paste for Ornaments. — Take some of the prepared paste, as

---

* An excellent work for the use of the ornamental confectioner is Page's "Acanthus," which may be obtained of any bookseller.

for the last, and work into it on the stone some very fine starch pow der, using equal quantities of starch and sugar.   This may also be made with rice flour, instead of starch.   These are chiefly used for pièces montées.   It may be moulded or modelled into any form, or cut out from figures or borders carved in wood, called gum-paste boards, using a little starch-powder to prevent its sticking whilst working it ; a little tied up in a small muslin bag is the handiest for use.   When you want to get the paste from the impressions in the boards, take a small piece of paste and press it at each end ; if it does not come out very readily, moisten the piece, and touch that in the impression at three or four places, which, being damp, adheres to it and draws it out.

Paste for gilding on. — Take some dissolved gum, as before, and make it into a paste with a little starch-powder to finish it ; or it may be made with some of the prepared sugar gum-paste, finishing it with starch-powder.

Papier Mâchée.—Take the cuttings of either white or brown paper, and boil them in water until reduced to a paste; press the water from it when cold enough, and pound it well in a mortar ; put it into a pan or glazed pipkin, with a little gum Arabic, Senegal, or common glue, made into rather a thick mucilage with water ; this is to give it tenacity ; place it on the fire and stir it until well incorporated ; if it is not stiff enough when cold, flour may be added to make it of the proper consistence ; it should be about the same substance as gum paste.   This may be used for forming the rocks of a pièce montée, or for vases, cassolettes, &c. ; in fact anything you desire may be made with it, as with gum paste ; it is very durable, not being easily broken, and is very light ; it is now much used, instead of compo sition, for the decorations of rooms and articles of furniture.   It is from this that paper trays, snuff boxes, &c., are manufactured, and it is much used in France for making various beautiful little ornaments for containing bon-bons, &c.   It may be moulded or modelled into any form, or cut from impressions in wood or plaster, &c.   When the object is dry, give it a coating of composition, made with parchment size, and whitening or lamp-black, mixed to the consistence of oil paint, according to the colour it is required.   Smooth it with glass paper, and paint or gild as wood, or japan it.*

To gild Gum Paste, &c.—Those articles which are gilt are seldom intended to be eaten, therefore first give them a coating of parchment size and whitening, as the papier mâchée, or paint them with oil colour.   When this is dry, brush over a coat of gold size, and let it remain until nearly dry, or so as it will stick to the fingers a little ; then take a small dry brush, termed by gilders a tip, rub a little

---

* For further particulars, and for the method of taking the impressions of moulds with composition, see the ' Guide to Trade—The Carver and Gilder,' Knight & Co., p. 53.

grease over the back of your hand, and pass the brush over it gently;
apply it to the gold leaf, which it will take up, and place it on the
part you intend to gild; blow on it to make it smooth; the gold leaf
may first be divided into small pieces with a knife on a leather pad or
cushion, to suit the size of your work; rub it over gently with a piece
of wool, to make it appear glossy. Those parts which have not taken
the gold, just breathe on, then apply a small piece of the leaf, and rub
again with the wool. If your piece is intended to be eaten, let the
paste be perfectly dry and smooth; then prepare some mucilage of
gum Arabic, strain it, and grind it well with an equal portion of white
sugar candy; lay it over the part you intend to gild with a stiff
brush; when dry, breathe on it, so as to moisten it, and gild as
before.

To Bronze Gum Paste.—Prepare your object, if not to be eaten, as
for gilding, giving it a coat of invisible green, prepared with turpentine, a little japan gold size, and a small portion of oil; when it is
nearly dry, dip a fitch pencil in some bronze powder, shake off the
loose pieces which hang about the brush, and apply it to the parts you
wish to assume the appearance of copper, which are in general the
most prominent.

Another method.—Smooth your finger with sand-paper, and give it
a coat of isinglass dissolved, or parchment size; when this is dry,
give it a coat of colour made as follows:—Take a sufficient quantity
of prepared indigo, with verditer blue, and a little spruce ochre or
saffron, in such proportions as to make a deep green; grind them together with white of egg and powdered sugar-candy, or with parchment size; give it a coat of this, and when nearly dry apply the
bronze as before.

On the Construction of Assiettes and Pièces Montées.—To be a profi-
cient in this part requires a general knowledge of the fine arts, particularly the principles of architecture; for without this, however well
your piece may be finished with regard to workmanship, it still remains a dull, heavy, unmeaning mass, having no proportion nor a
particle of true design in it. I have seen many pieces, and some in
the principal shops, with these defects, although otherwise well exe-
cuted. My limits will not allow me to enter into the details necessary to illustrate this part, therefore the artist must refer to books on
the subject; but in the absence of these it is best to work from some
correct drawing, which, with the few notes I shall subjoin, may serve
for general purposes.

There are many prevailing styles or orders of architecture, as the
Egyptian, Grecian, Roman, Saxon, Norman, Gothic, &c. The Gothic
is the most beautiful, being pointed, and is generally used for cathe-
drals and churches. The Norman is plain and simple, with semicircular arches. The Saxon is after the same style, into which are
introduced some ornamental workings. The Egyptian is more flat
and square, embellished with hieroglyphics. In the Grecian and

Roman architecture there are five orders, viz., Tuscan, Doric, Ionic, Corinthian, and Composite; and a building may be denominated Ionic, Corinthian, &c., merely from its ornaments. The number of columns, windows, &c., may be the same in either order, but varied in their proportions. The height of the columns in each is, — for the Tuscan, seven times its diameter; Doric, eight; Ionic, nine; Corinthian, ten; Composite, ten. The Tuscan is quite plain, without any ornament whatever; the Doric is distinguished by the channels and projecting intervals in the frieze, called tryglyphs; the Ionic by the ornaments of its capital, which are spiral, and called volutes; the Corinthian by the superior height of its capital, and its being ornamented with leaves, which support very small volutes; the Composite has also a tall capital, with leaves, but is distinguished from the Corinthian by having the large volutes of the Ionic capital. The Grecian and Roman orders differ in some respects as to the style of each, but for particulars refer to works on the subject. These orders are adopted for buildings, with various modifications, in most parts of the world.

The Chinese have a peculiar kind of style, which needs no description, as it is generally represented in this country on our delft ware, &c. The Swiss style, which is something of the Gothic, is very well adapted for pièces montées, as well as the Doric, Ionic, and Corinthian orders, they being more light and elegant.

Of Pièces Montées.—These are in general made to represent buildings of all descriptions, fountains, trophies, vases, cups, helmets, the last being generally mounted on pedestals and filled with flowers, fruit, &c.; also rocks, bridges, fortifications, &c. &c., the building, &c., being generally made with gum-paste, confectioners' or almond pastes. The bodies of rocks may be formed with pieces of rock sugar, cakes, biscuits, &c., of all descriptions, being fixed together with caramel sugar; those not intended to be eaten may be made with papier mâchée and common gum-paste; the rocks or bottoms of these are often formed with pieces of cork, flocks, and paper, the surface being afterwards covered with a coating of very thin icing, which is applied with a brush.

To construct your pieces with accuracy, first cut out your intended design in stout paper, in suitable parts to be put together; then roll out the paste thin on a marble stone; lay your pattern on it, and cut your paste to it with a small sharp-pointed knife; let it dry, and fix it together with some dissolved gum, or a little gum-paste made rather thin with water. Cut your ornaments or decorations from pasteboards; let them dry a few minutes, and fix them in their proper places. Water may be represented with a piece of looking-glass, and falling water with silver web or spun glass.

Biscuit Paste to imitate Marble Rocks, &c, for Pièces Montées. — Prepare some paste as for Savoy cakes (see p. 94); take one-third of the mixture, and add to it some dissolved chocolate; stir the whole well together, and divide into two equal portions; to one part add some more of the mixture, when you will have a light and dark

brown; mix together some prepared cochineal or carmine and infu
sion of saffron, to make a dark orange, and stir this into another portion of paste; divide it, and add to one part some more of the paste,
which will give a light and dark orange; butter or paper a square
tin, and put in a spoonful of each coloured paste in rotation, spreading it with the spoon so as it may appear in layers, beginning with
the dark colours, and so alternately until the whole is used; or one-
half of each may be put into another tin, and mixed all together, so
that it may appear in veins; bake it in a moderate oven, and when
cold cut it into pieces as it is required, to represent pieces of rock,
marble, &c. For variety, the paste may be coloured with spinach
green, infusion of saffron, red, and blue, and either put in layers or
mixed together as before.

Pâte d'Office, or Confectioners' Paste. — Take one pound and a
quarter of fine flour, and ten ounces of loaf sugar sifted through a
fine sieve; make a bay, and put in it a sufficient quantity of the yolks
or whites of eggs, or whole eggs, to make it into a moderate stiff
paste; work it well, and make it quite smooth; let it remain covered
over for a short time, that it may get mellow. If this paste is required white and delicate, use the whites only of the eggs. This is
used for the frame-work or building of the pièces montées, or for the
bottom or foundation on which you build your biscuits, sugar, &c.
Roll it out on an even board or marble slab until it is about one-sixth
of an inch in thickness, or more, according to the weight it has to
bear. Dust your sheet, and roll it on the pin; then lay or roll it over
a baking-plate slightly buttered; press out any air-bladders which
may be underneath, and prick it with the point of a sharp-pointed
knife in a few places; lay on your patterns, cut it out to the desired
form, and bake in a moderate oven; or it may be cut out when the
paste is half baked, and finish baking it afterwards; or it may be
dried in the stove instead of being baked. If it should be blistered
when it is taken from the oven, put it immediately on an even board,
and place another on it; remove it when it is cold, and it will be
quite straight.

This paste may be made with the addition of half an ounce of dissolved gum-dragon, pounding it well in a mortar, and using less eggs.
Each of these may be coloured to any desired tint, when it should be
dried in a stove instead of being baked. Fix the parts together, when
finished, with some of the same paste made thin with dissolved gum,
or with caramel sugar; ornament it with spun sugar, or with coloured
sugar-sands. (See Coloured Sugar).

From this paste, or almond paste, may be made cottages, temples,
fountains, pyramids, castles, bridges, hermits'-cells, vases, or any
other required forms, which are to be made in different pieces and put
together afterwards, or formed in moulds, and either baked or dried
in the stove.

Assiettes Montées, or dressed plates. These are composed of pieces

of wire of different sizes to suit the dimensions of the piece, which
is bound round with silver or tissue paper, and fastened with paste.
These wires, after they are fashioned to the desired figure, are fixed
with binding wire, and the whole is finished with stout Bristol-board
or card paper, ornamented gold borders and papers, and decorated
with gum paste. They are placed in the centre of the table, with
bon-bons, &c.

On Modelling.—This art is most important to the confectioner. It
is not so difficult to accomplish as is generally supposed; it only requires patience and perseverance, with a close attention to the proportions and orders of nature. A few modelling tools, and facility in
handling the paste, is all that is requisite to become an expert model-
ler. The form of the body must first be made with the fingers, the
more minute parts with the tools and a pair of scissors; the last is
very useful for dividing the fingers on the hands and the toes of a
human figure. The proportions necessary to form it are these:—the
whole length of a human being is six times the length of his feet,
eight times of his head (that is, from the crown to the chin), ten
times of his face, or the distance from the crown to the mouth; the
thumb is as long as the nose or the biggest joint of the middle finger;
the fore finger is shorter than the third, and the little finger is shorter
than the third by one joint; the width of the wrist is as long as the
thumb, end about a quarter; this varies; the ear is also the length
of the nose, its breadth half its length; the arm is three times the
length of the head, or four faces; the leg, from the knee-joint to the
bottom of the foot, measures two heads and a-half; the foot, which is
one-sixth of the human stature, if divided into three parts, will contain first the toes from the top of the large one to the lowest joint of
the little one; next the middle of the foot, and lastly the heel and
instep. There is also a slight difference between the proportions of a
male and female. In infancy and very early youth the form is very
much alike in both sexes. The head is oval, very much extended
backwards, with the forehead and top of the head comparatively flat;
the jaw-bones are short and have little depth; the bones of the nose
are short and flat; in the male subject, the elevation of the frontal
sinuses at the eyebrows, which characterizes the male head, is wanting; and the neck is very small in proportion to the head. In old age
the cheeks and mouth fall in, because of the wasting of the teeth;
the nose and chin approach each other; the fat is absorbed, and the
muscles shrink, which covers the surface with wrinkles; and in time,
the bones too are wasted, and the figure bends beneath its own
weight. With these directions proceed to model the human figure,
referring to anatomical plates for the position of the muscles, &c.
When the figure is complete, proceed to dress it in any style or cos-
tume you may fancy, making it from the same paste, and colouring
it, giving the figure any attitude you may think proper, but always
prefer the graceful, avoiding the stiff and awkward. The modelling
of animals and birds is on the same principle, the wings of the latter

being pushed or cut in moulds or pasteboards. Flowers are mostly done with cutters in the form of the leaf of the flowers you would wish to represent ; form the calyx in a mould, and fasten it on a piece of wire ; fix the leaves on the calyx to imitate nature, and colour them accordingly.

1.   2.   3.   4.

Modelling Tools.—No. 1 is termed the rose-stick, the thin flat end being used for forming the leaves of roses out of modelling wax by flattening a piece of it on a table until it is of the required form and size; the other end is used for fluting and making borders.

No. 2 is by some termed a foot tool, being used for forming the edges and borders to wax baskets, the circular end being necessary for working underneath any part, or circular mouldings, and also for the paws of animals.

No. 3. The curved thin end is used as a cutting tool, and for the formation of leaves; and the opposite end for fluting.

No. 4 serves as a gouge, and is used in the formation of leaves for flowers.

The curves of each tool are also requisite for different purposes in modelling, and for forming the raised and depressed parts in the human figure, animals, &c. They should be made of beech, as it relieves better when used about fat or modelling wax. There are many others, but these will be found quite sufficient for most purposes, with the dotting or pointing tool, which a common skewer, or piece of round pointed stick will supply its place. The tool usually made for this purpose has a concave or semicircular hollow at the thick end, for making beading, or else with a flat round end, similar to a tambour needle; the last being used for working up the leaves of roses, &c., in the hollow of the hand, when they are made of gum-paste.

Modelling Wax.—This is made of white wax, which is melted and mixed with lard to make it malleable. In working it, the tools and the board or stone are moistened with water to prevent its adhering; it may be coloured to any desired tint with dry colour.

SECTION XXII.—ON COLOURS.

MANY of the colours prepared for use in this art come more properly under the denomination of dyes, alum and cream of tartar being used as a mordant; and many of them are prepared in the same manner as for dyeing. One of the principal colours requisite for the confectioner's use is coccinella, or cochineal. The sorts generally sold are the black, silver, foxy, and the granille. The insect is of two species, the fine and the wild cochineal; the fine differs from the wild in size, and is also covered with a white mealy powder. The best is of a deep mulberry colour, with a white powder between the wrinkles, and a bright red within. A great deal of adulteration is practised with this article, both at home and abroad; it is on this account that persons prefer the silver grain, because it cannot be so well sophisticated. Good cochineal should be heavy, dry, and more or less of a silvery colour, and without smell.

To prepare Cochineal.—Pound an ounce of cochineal quite fine, and put it into a pint of river water with a little potash or soda, and let it boil; then add about a quarter of an ounce powdered alum, the same of cream of tartar, and boil for ten minutes; if it is required for keeping, add two or three ounces of powdered loaf sugar.

Carmine.—Reduce one ounce of cochineal to a fine powder, add to it six quarts of clear rain or filtered water, as for cochineal. Put this into a large tin saucepan, or a copper one tinned, and let it boil for three minutes, then add twenty-five grains of alum, and let it boil two minutes longer; take it off the fire to cool; when it is blood warm pour off the clear liquor into shallow vessels, and put them by to settle for two days, covering them with paper to keep out the dust. In case the carmine has not separated properly, add a few drops of a solution of tin, or a solution of green vitriol, which is tin dissolved in muriatic acid, or the following may be substituted:—one ounce and a half of spirit of nitre, three scruples of sal-ammoniac, three scruples of tin dissolved in a bottle, and use a few drops as required. When the carmine has settled, decant off the clear which is liquid rouge. The first sediment is Florence lake, which remove, and dry the carmine for use. This preparation is by far superior to the first, for in this the same colour is obtained as before, which is the liquid rouge, the other and more expensive parts being invariably thrown away. The carmine can be obtained by the first process, as can be seen if the whole is poured into a clear bottle and allowed to settle, when the carmine will be deposited in a layer of bright red near the bottom. It produces about half an ounce of carmine.

Yellow.—Infuse saffron in warm water, and use it for colouring any thing that is eatable. The English hay-saffron is the best; it is taken from the tops of the pistils of the crocus flower; it is frequently adulterated with the flowers of marygolds or safflower, which is known as the bastard saffron, and is pressed into thin cakes with oil. Good saffron has a strong agreeable odour, and an aromatic taste. Gum paste and other articles which are not eaten may be coloured with gamboge dissolved in warm water.

Prussian Blue may be used instead of indigo, if preferred, but must be used sparingly.

Sap Green.—This is prepared from the fruit of the buckthorn, and is purgative.

Spinach Green.—This is perfectly harmless and will answer most purposes. Wash and drain a sufficient quantity of spinach, pound it well in a mortar, and squeeze the pounded leaves in a coarse cloth to extract all the juice; put it in a pan and set it on a good fire, and stir it occasionally until it curdles, which will be when it is at the boiling point; then take it off and strain off the water with a fine sieve; the residue left is the green; dry it and rub it through a lawn sieve. This is only fit for opaque bodies, such as ices, creams, or syrups.

Another green is made with a mixture of saffron or gamboge, and prepared indigo; the lighter the green the more yellow must be used.

Vermilion and Cinnabar are preparations of mercury, and should never be used; they are of a lively red colour, but carmine will answer most purposes instead.

Bole Ammoniac.—There is also the French and German bole. These earths are of a pale red, and possess alexipharmic qualities; they are frequently used in confectionary for painting and gilding.

Umber.—This is of a blackish brown colour; it is an earth found near Cologne.

Bistre.—This is an excellent light brown colour prepared from wood soot.

These browns are harmless, but sugar may be substituted for them to any shade required by continuing the boiling after it has passed the degree of caramel until it is burnt, when it gives a black-brown, but water may be mixed with it so as to lessen the shades. Dissolved chocolate may also be substituted in some cases for the brown colours.

Black.—Blue-black is powdered charcoal, or ivory black, which is obtained from the smoke of burnt ivory; but bone black is generally substituted instead; either of these may be used, but are only required for painting gum paste, when not intended to be eaten.

Obtain any of these colours in fine powder, and mix them with some dissolved gum Arabic, a little water, and a pinch of powdered sugar candy; mix them to the required consistence for painting. For sugars they must be used in a liquid state, and be added before it has attained the proper degree; it may also be used in the same manner for ices, creams, &c., and for icings it can be used either way.

THE SHADES PRODUCED BY A MIXTURE OF COLOURS.

Purple.—Mix carmine or cochineal, and a small portion of indigo.

Lilac.—The same, making the blue predominate.

Orange.—Yellow, with a portion of red.

Gold.—The same, but the yellow must be more in excess.

Lemon.—Use a solution of saffron.

Green.—Blue and yellow.

SECTION XXIII.——DISTILLATION.

THIS art is of great importance to a confectioner, as it enables him to make his own oils, waters, and spirits for liqueurs and ratafias, instead of purchasing at a high rate those vile adulterations which are often sold.

The still or apparatus for distilling consists of a cucurbit, which is a copper pot or boiler, and contains the wash, dregs, or infusions to be distilled. A cover, with a large tapering neck or pipe in the cen tre, is fixed on, and a continuation of small pipe, made either of tin or pewter, of several feet in length, is bent into a spiral form, and termed the worm. This is placed in a tub containing water, which is fastened on to the end of the neck. The joints or crevices are luted, to prevent evaporation, with a paste made of linseed meal, or equal portions of slacked lime or whitening, flour and salt, moistened with water, and spread on rags or pieces of bladder, when it is applied to the joints and crevices. The water in the tub where the worm is should be kept quite cold, except in distilling oil of anise-seeds; and for this purpose a tap or cock should be placed about half-way down the tub, that the top of the water may be drawn off when it is warm. Again fill it with cold water, and keep coarse cloths dipped in cold water to put round the alembic or still in case it should boil too fast. It is by these means that the steam or vapour which rises with the heat is condensed, and runs out at the end of the pipe in a small stream. If the operation is well conducted, it should never exceed this. When the phlegm arises, which is a watery insipid liquor, the receiver must be withdrawn, for if *a drop* of it should run in, it must be cohobated, that is, re-distilled, as it will thicken the spirit and spoil the taste.

The still should not be filled above three parts full, to prevent it rising over the neck, should it happen to boil violently, as in this case it would spoil what is already drawn, which must be re-distilled.

ON ESSENTIAL OILS.

To obtain these from plants or peels, the articles should be infused for two or three days, or even longer, in a sufficient quantity of cold water, until it has fully penetrated the pores of the materials. For this purpose roots should be cut into thin slices, barks reduced to a coarse powder, and seeds slightly bruised; those of soft and loose texture require to be infused two or three days, the harder and more compact a week or two, whilst some tender herbs and plants require to be distilled directly. After the solvent has fully penetrated, distil it with an open fire; that is, a fire under the still like a common washing copper, which immediately strikes the bottom. Regulate the fire so as to make it boil as speedily as possible, and that the oil may continue to distil freely during the whole process; for the longer it is submitted to an unnecessary heat without boiling, a greater portion of the oil is mixed with the water than there would otherwise be. The oil comes over the water, and either sinks to the bottom or swims on the top, according as it is lighter or heavier than that fluid. What comes over at first is more fragrant than that towards the end, which is thicker, and should be re-distilled by a gentle heat, when it leaves a resinous matter behind.

All essential oils, after they are distilled, should be suffered to stand some days in open bottles or vessels, loosely covered with paper to keep out the dust, until they have lost their disagreeable fiery odour, and become quite limpid: put them into small bottles, and keep them quite full in a cold place. The light oils pass over the swan neck of the common still, but the heavier ones will not so readily, therefore a large low head is preferable ; the heavier oils are those from cloves, allspice, cinnamon, &c., or such as contain a portion of resin.

Some plants yield three times as much oil, if gathered when the flowers begin to fall off,—as lavender ; others when young, before they have sent forth any flowers,—as sage ; and others when the flowers begin to appear,—as thyme.

All fragrant herbs yield a large portion of oil when produced in dry soils and warm summers. Herbs and flowers give out a larger quantity of oil after they have been partly dried in a dry shady place. Four pounds of the leaves of the dried mint yield one ounce of oil, but six pounds of fresh leaves only three drachms and a-half. This oil is more fine and bright when rectified—that is, re-distilled.

After the distillation of one oil, the worm should be carefully cleansed, by passing a little spirit of wine through it, before another is proceeded with.

A great quantity of oil is wasted by confectioners when they pre-serve their lemon and orange peels by boiling them in open vessels instead of a still ; what is saved by this means alone would soon repay the expense of the apparatus.

DISTILLED WATERS.

These are obtained in a similar manner to the oils, with a high narrow-necked still, and differ from them by the oil being retained or united with the water. Plants for this purpose should be gathered fresh on a dry day, as the water drawn from them in this state is more aromatic when they are dry ; for the oil is mixed with an aque-ous fluid in the plant, which concretes and separates in drying.

Herbs should be bruised and steeped for a day in about three times their quantity of water when green, but considerably more when dry ; but at all times sufficient water should be added that some may be left to prevent the herbs or flowers being burnt to the bottom of the still. After all the water is drawn, the distillation should continue so long as any taste or smell of the ingredients comes over ; and the fire should be so regulated that the water may run in a small con tinued stream.

If a superior article is required, it must be re-distilled by a gentle heat, with the addition of a little pure spirit (about one-twentieth part) which has not got any bad smell.

Orange-Flower Water.—The leaves of orange flowers three pounds, water three pints.

Rose Water. — As orange flower, using either the damask or pale single rose. Neither the purgative quality of the damask, nor the astringent quality of red roses, rises in distillation, but is contained in the water left in the still.

Cinnamon Water. — Cinnamon one pound, water two gallons. Bruise or break the spice, and infuse it in water for two days. Some consider it sufficient to simmer the spice in the still for half an hour, putting back what comes over, and filtering the whole when cold through a flannel bag or blotting paper.

Peppermint Water. — Dried herb one pound and a half, or green herb three pounds, to a gallon of water.

Lemon-Peel Water.—Two pounds of fresh peel to the gallon.

Black-Cherry Water.—Twelve pounds of ripe fruit to a gallon of water. Bruise the fruit in a mortar so as to break the stones, that the flavour of the kernel may be obtained.

Angelica, star, anise-seed, caraway, lavender, rosemary, myrtle, vanilla, raspberry, strawberry, and all other waters, are made in the same manner; the first half of the water which comes over is the best and strongest.

SPIRITS FOR LIQUEURS.

Spirits and alcohol are obtained by the distillation of fermented articles. The peculiar taste of each depends on the essential oil of the article from which it is prepared being held in solution: therefore, by knowing the nature of its oil, alcohol may be made to imitate any desired spirit. A few drops of nitric ether added to malt spirit will impart to it the flavour of cognac brandy; and two scruples of benzoic acid, mixed with one quart of rum, will give it the taste of arrack. Brandy is generally recommended for the use of the confectioner in making spirits for liqueurs, but a superior article may be made with less expense from rectified spirits of wine, or pure spirit which has neither taste nor smell, as the spirit afterwards drawn will only have the flavour of the articles with which it is required to be impregnated. Rectified spirits may be obtained from the dregs of beer, cider, ale or wine, suitable for any purpose, as well as from brandy.

Spirits rise in the still with less heat than watery infusions, therefore it is best to distil by means of the bain-marie, that is, by the still being placed in another vessel containing water. This method is more safe, as it prevents accidents, and the articles from being burnt.

Common spirits may be deprived of their impurities by mixing them with an equal quantity of water, and distilling them by a gentle heat, or in a water-bath. Continue the operation until the phlegm arises, which will appear milky and is of a nauseous taste. A great quantity of the oil which it retained will remain in the water. If the spirit was very impure, a second rectification may be necessary, as before. A very pure and tasteless spirit may be obtained by mixing with the spirit, after rectification, one-fourth of its weight of pure dry salt of wormwood or tartar. Let it stand a little time in a *gentle heat*, and distil in the bain-marie. A small portion of alum being added, prevents any of the salt being brought over with the spirit. The result is pure alcohol. It may be reduced to proof spirit by mixing twenty ounces of alcohol with seventeen of water, by weight.

Distilled Spirituous Waters for Liqueurs.—Orange, rose, pink, jessamine, and all other flowers, are made by adding eight pounds of the leaves or petals of the flowers to a gallon of pure proof spirit. Put them in a cold cellar or ice-house to infuse for a week. Distil in the bain-marie to dryness. If they are distilled on an open gentle fire, water should be added to the articles when they are put on the fire, so as to prevent their being burnt.

Lavender, mint, rosemary, angelica, the yellow rind of lemon and orange peels, and bergamot, lemon, vanilla, ginger, and orris-root for violet, and other herbs, are made by adding two pounds of the plant, &c., partly dried, to a gallon of pure proof spirit. Let it steep in a jar close covered for twelve or fourteen days in a cool place, and distil in the bain-marie. Myrtle and balm-*melissæ*, one pound to the gallon. If any of the waters appear rather turbid when they are first drawn, they will become clear and bright by standing a few days. Filter them through blotting paper-placed in a glass or earthenware funnel over a bottle to receive them.

Strawberries, raspberries, &c., sixteen pounds to the gallon.

Cinnamon, coriander, caraways, cloves, &c., are made by adding one pound of the bruised seed or spice to the gallon of proof spirit. Cardamoms four ounces, nutmegs and mace three ounces to the gallon.

Hungary Water, or Aqua Reginæ.—Fresh gathered rosemary flowers in full bloom, four pounds to the gallon of pure proof spirit. It may also be made with the addition of one pound of each of marjoram and lavender flowers, and two quarts more of spirit. Distil immediately. Half a pound of sage leaves, and two ounces of ginger, are recommended as an excellent addition by foreign writers.

Maraschino de Zara.— Morello cherries nine pounds, black wild cherries seven pounds, or sixteen pounds of Morello cherries,* one pint and a-quarter of Kirchenwasser, spirit of roses one ounce and a-half, spirit of orange flowers one ounce and a-half, of jessamine a quarter of an ounce, peach or cherry leaves one pound and a-quarter; pick the stalks from the cherries and press out their juice, pound the stones and skins with the leaves in a mortar, and steep all together for a fortnight,—some only filter the infusion,—and add to it four pounds and a-half of treble-refined sugar; dissolve and strain through a jelly-bag; but a superior spirit may be obtained by the addition of four quarts of rectified proof spirit; distil with the bain-marie, and rectify.

---

* Genuine Maraschino is the spirit of Morello cherries, as Kirchenwasser is of black cherries. Maraschino may also be made from gooseberries. Ripe gooseberries 102 pounds; black cherry leaves bruised, 12 pounds; ferment as Kirchenwasser; distil and rectify it.

Kirchenwasser.—Get some small black cherries and a few Morello cherries quite ripe, take off their stalks and put them in a cask with the head off, cover the top or surface of the cherries with mortar or wood ashes mixed to a consistence with water, let them stand for six weeks or two months, during which time they will ferment, then take off the covering and distil them.

Eau Divine.—Essence of bergamont and lemon, of each one drachm, rectified spirit one gallon, fresh balm leaves two ounces; distil with the bain-marie; add orange-flower water five ounces. The liquor is made by adding to this four pounds of treble refined sugar, dissolved in two gallons of water.

Eau de Cologne.—Spirit of rosemary two quarts, essence of bergamot four ounces, balm water two quarts, essence of cédrats and citrons four ounces, neroli two drachms, rosemary two ounces, spirits of wine ten quarts; draw fourteen quarts.

Balm water two pints and a-quarter, spirit of rosemary three pounds and a-half, oil of rosemary one drachm, essence of lemon three drachms, of cédrats two drachms, of neroli two drachms and a-half, of bergamot three drachms, rectified spirit twelve pounds, distil in the bain-marie, and keep in a cool place for some time.

Curaçao.—This is a species of wild or bitter orange; the dried peel may be obtained from the chemists; the yellow peel of Seville oranges, dried and powdered, will answer as well; use one pound to the gallon of rum or rectified spirit, and distil as the others.

Eau de Mélisse des Carmes.—Spirit of balm eight pints, spirit of lemon and citron four pints; spirit of nutmegs, musk, and coriander, of each two pints, spirit of thyme, cinnamon, anise-seed, marjoram, hyssop, green-verdigris, or the vitriol of iron, sage, angelica-root, and cloves, of each one pint; distil, and keep in an ice-house for twelve months. Supposed to be the original recipe of the barefooted Carmelites, now in possession of the Company of Apothecaries of Paris.

The English Method.—Fresh balm leaves four ounces, fresh lemon-peel two ounces (the yellow rind), coriander seeds and nutmegs, of each one ounce, angelica-root, cinnamon, and cloves, of each half an ounce, rectified spirit two pounds, brandy two pounds, powder the dry ingredients, and steep the whole in a close vessel with the spirit for four or five days. Two pints of rectified spirit and one pint of balm-water may be used instead of the spirit and brandy; distil in the bain-marie nearly to dryness; re-distil and keep it for some time in a cold cellar or ice-house. This is an elegant and beautiful cordial.

Spirit of Coffee.—One pound of the best Mocha coffee, fresh roasted and ground, add to it one gallon of rectified proof spirit, let it infuse for a week, and distil in the bain-marie.

Spirit of bitter Almonds.—One pound of blanched almonds, one gallon of proof spirit; pound the almonds quite fine with a little water, to prevent their oiling, add them to the spirit with an ounce of bruised angelica-root, steep for a week, and distil in the bain-marie.

Spirit of Tea.—Four ounces of the best tea to a gallon of rectified proof spirit, pour a little cold water on the tea and let it infuse for three or four hours, add it to the spirit, and distil it in a week.

Escubac—Usquebaugh.—Saffron one ounce, catechu three ounces, ambergris half a grain, dates without their kernels, and raisins, each three ounces, jujubes six ounces, anise-seed, cloves, mace, and coriander seed one drachm, cinnamon two drachms, proof spirit six quarts, pound the ingredients, infuse for a week and distil. The whole of these spirituous distilled waters are for making liquors and for flavouring ices, liqueurs, bon-bons, drops, &c., or anything in which liquors are introduced.

LIQUEURS.

These are made by mixing equal proportions of any of the spirits, water, and sugar together, that is, one pint of spirit, one pint of water, one pound of the treble-refined sugar; dissolve the sugar in the water, add it to the spirit, and filter through blotting-paper; being perfectly clear and colourless when drawn, they require to be coloured of the same tint as the articles from which they were extracted, and for this purpose none but those which are perfectly harmless should be employed, as prepared cochineal, infusion of saffron, burnt sugars or indigo.

RATAFIAS.

These are liqueurs made by the infusion of the ingredients in spirits, and are similarly composed to the spirituous waters, but instead of being distilled they are simply filtered, and sugar is added to them.

Ratafia de Café.—Fresh roasted Mocha coffee ground, one pound, proof spirit one gallon, loaf sugar one pound and a half; infuse for a week, string it every other day, filter, bottle, and cork close.

Ratafia de Cacao.—Cacao of Caracca one pound, West India cocoa nuts eight ounces, proof spirit one gallon, roast the nuts and bruise them, add them to the spirit and infuse for fourteen days, stirring them occasionally, filter and add thirty drops of essence of vanilla and two pounds of sugar.

Ratafia des Noyaux.—Half a pound of bitter almonds, half a pound of sweet almonds, proof spirit one gallon, (peach or apricot kernels may be used instead of the bitter almonds), three pounds of loaf sugar; beat the almonds fine with part of the sugar, steep the whole together for twelve or fourteen days, and filter; this liqueur will be much improved if rectified spirit is reduced to proof with the juice of apricots or peaches.

Ratafia of Cherries.—Morello cherries eight pounds, black cherries eight pounds, raspberries and red or white currants of each two pounds, coriander-seeds three ounces, cinnamon half an ounce, mace half an ounce, proof spirit one gallon; press out the juice from the fruit, take one-half of the stones of the cherries and pound them with the spices, and add two pounds and a half of sugar, steep for a month and filter.

Ratafia des Cassis.—Ripe black currants six pounds, cloves half a drachm, cinnamon one drachm, black currant leaves one pound and a half, Morello cherries two pounds, sugar five pounds, proof spirit eight quarts; bruise the spice, infuse a fortnight, filter, and bottle.

Ratafia of Raspberries.—Raspberries quite ripe eight pounds, proof spirit one gallon, quarter of an ounce of cinnamon and cloves, steep for fourteen days, stirring it occasionally. Currants and strawberries are made the same.

Ratafia des Fleurs des Oranges.—Fresh orange-flowers two pounds, proof spirit one gallon, sugar two pounds; infuse for eight or ten hours.

Ratafia d'Œillets.—The petals of clove pinks, with the white parts pulled off, four pounds, cinnamon and cloves twenty-five grains, proof spirit one gallon, sugar three pounds. Infuse for a month, filter, and bottle.

Ratafia d'Angelique.—Angelica seeds one ounce, angelica stalks four ounces, bitter almonds four ounces, one drachm each of cinnamon and cloves, proof spirit six quarts, loaf sugar four pounds. Blanch and pound the almonds with some of the sugar, or a little water; pound the other ingredients a little, and bruise the stalks. Infuse for a month, stirring it occasionally. Filter and bottle.

Vespetro.—Coriander seed one ounce, angelica seed two ounces, fennel and anise-seed of each two drachms, two lemons, two oranges, the zest of two citrons, two quarts of rectified spirit and two pounds of sugar, caraway seeds four grains. Bruise the ingredients, pare off the yellow rind of the lemons and oranges, and squeeze the juice. Dissolve the sugar in a pint of water. Infuse the whole together for fourteen days. Strain, filter, and bottle.

Chrême de Barbade.—The yellow rind of three oranges and three lemons, cinnamon four ounces, mace two drachms, cloves one drachm, rum nine quarts, fresh balm leaves six ounces. Infuse and distil in the bain-marie, or strain; add an equal quantity of sugar with water

Chrême d'Orange. — Thirty-six sweet oranges, sliced, tincture of saffron one ounce and four drachms, orange-flower water four pints, rectified spirits two gallons, water eighteen quarts, loaf sugar eighteen pounds. Dissolve the sugar in the water: mix the other articles and infuse for a fortnight. Filter and bottle.

Ratafia d'Anis.—Star anise-seed four ounces, proof spirit one gal lon. Infuse for a fortnight; add two pounds of sugar, or a pint and a-half of syrup, and a little essence of vanilla.

Ratafia de Brout des Noix.—Young walnuts, when the shells are not formed, number eighty, mace, cinnamon, and cloves, of each half a drachm, proof spirit one gallon. Pound the nuts in a mortar, add them and the spice to the spirit, with two pounds of sugar. Infuse for two months, stirring it occasionally; press out the liquor through a cloth. Filter and bottle.

SECTION XXV.—THE STOVE OR HOT CLOSET.

THIS is a useful and indispensable appendage in confectionary; it is generally constructed like a cupboard in the recess of a wall. The walls or sides should be composed of bricks, or wood lined with tin or sheet iron, to retain the heat, with pieces of wood nailed or fastened in the sides, about four inches asunder, to form a groove for trays or boards to rest on, which is necessary for the drying of lozenges, comfits, bon-bons, &c.; there should also be a few strong shifting shelves made either of small bars of round iron or wood, like a grating, on which candy pots or sieves may be placed; the grooves for these should be so constructed as to be capable of inclination so as to drain off the syrup from the candy pots without taking them from the shelves; the door should be made to shut close, with a small door at the top to let out any excess of heat. I have before remarked that it may be heated by means of many of the modern stoves. At places where the oven is heated with wood, furze, &c., a common iron pot or crock with three legs is filled with the live embers, or it may be filled with burning charcoal and covered with wood ashes, which is replenished night and morning, which gives the heat required.

THE PASTRY-COOK.

~~~~~~~~~~~~~~

INTRODUCTION.

We now came to a very important, because a very difficult, branch of the art of baking, whether exercised as a profession, or by private individuals, namely the manufacturing of what are technically called "*fancy goods.*" The reader scarcely need be informed, that this term includes all those varieties of baked manufactured eatables, in which such ingredients as sugar, eggs, spice, and butter, are used, with many other not necessary to enumerate here.

It ought to be observed, that the following directions for making the kind of goods alluded to, have been all *tested*, and found to be so exceedingly accurate as to proportions, that a deviation in a quantity so small as an egg, or even half an egg, will deteriorate the quality of the article. These directions are not generally known in the trade, and out of the trade they are entirely, we believe, unknown. They will be found, therefore, a valuable acquisition to those ladies who manage their own domestic affairs, and who are in the habit of making little *knick-knacks* for their children, or their dessert tables.

Previous to giving the directions in question, it will be necessary for our readers to be made acquainted with the mode of preparing certain articles, which are more or less employed in the manufacturing fancy goods. We are aware that there are many private individuals who would object to use the preparation called "honey-water," as well as that called "prepared treacle," on the ground of their consisting chiefly of drugs. As regards, however, the use of carbonate of ammonia (honey-water), it may be safely affirmed, that there is, in small quantities, nothing unhealthy in it, but on the contrary. The truth however is, the carbonate of ammonia used in biscuits, &c., is volatilized by the heat of baking, and of course it all escapes. Its operation is therefore mechanical, and the only effect it has upon the biscuit is to make it light.

With regard to the article called prepared treacle, which consists of treacle, alum, and pearlash, we have to observe, that alum taken in considerable quantities is decidedly unwholesome, it being of a powerfully astringent nature; but in the very small quantity here

prescribed, and considering that treacle is an asperient, and will consequently counteract the effects of the alum, we should say, that
there can be no harm in using it. Pearlash, being an alkali, we
should consider rather beneficial than otherwise, as it would prevent
the treacle of the ginger-bread turning acid on the stomach.

Having made these preliminary observations, we shall at once
proceed to give directions for making those preparations used in
pastry and fancy goods. The break alluded to in making fancy biscuits, is an instrument similar to that used in manufacturing ship-
biscuits, but of course of much smaller dimensions.

BLANCHED ALMONDS, ICING, PREPARED TREACLE, AND RENNET.

Blanched Almonds.—Cover your almonds with water, in a stew-
pan; set the pan on the fire, and strain them off as soon as the water
begins to boil, by which means the skins will peel off easily; put
them under the oven for a night, in a sieve, and they will be dry and
fit for use.

Icing for a Cake.—Take one pound of double-refined sugar,
pound it fine, and sift it through a lawn sieve; then beat the whites
of three eggs in a very clean pan, with a whisk, till they are a strong
froth, and hang round the pan, leaving the bottom clear; then, with
a wooden spoon, beat in your sugar, a little at a time, with about a
tea-spoonful of lemon-juice—beat it till it becomes a nice thick smooth
batter, and will hang round the pan to any thickness you may choose
to spread it. Then, when your cake is nearly cold, spread your
icing nicely over the top, and round the sides, with a pallet-knife; let
it stand in a warm place, where it will be safe from hurt, and it will
soon dry.

Prepared Treacle.—Dissolve two ounces of alum in a quarter of a
pint of boiling water, and stir it into seven pounds of treacle; then
dissolve four ounces of American pearlash in a quarter of a pint of
cold water, and well incorporate it with the treacle by stirring.

Rennet.—Milk is turned into curds and whey by means of rennet,
which is the stomach of a calf taken out as soon as it is killed, well
cleansed from its contents, then scoured inside and rubbed with salt,
when thoroughly salted, it is stretched on a stick to dry. A bit of
this is to be soaked in boiling water for several hours, and the liquid
put in milk-warm from the cow, or made of that warmth. Use alone
can prescribe the exact quantity: never use more than enough to turn
it, as it hardens the curd. The gizzard skin of fowls and turkey may
be prepared in the same way, and answer the same purpose.

FANCY BISCUITS.

Abernethy Biscuits.—(See Seed Biscuits.)

American.—Rub half a pound of butter into four pounds of flour, add a full pint of milk, or water; well wet them up; break your dough well, and bake them in a hot oven.

Brighton.—Take one pound and a quarter of good moist sugar, and roll it till it is fine; then pass it through a sieve with two pounds and a half of flour; rub in two ounces of butter; make a hole in the middle; strew in a few caraway seeds; pour in half a pint of honey-water, and a quarter of a pint of milk; beat it well with your hand till about half the flour is incorporated; then mix it together; roll it out in thin sheets; cut them out, and place them on your buttered tins about two inches apart; wash with a little beer; and bake them in a good steady heat.

Buttered.—Rub one pound of butter into seven pounds of flour; wet up with one quart of warm water, and half a pint of good yeast; break down smooth; prove your dough well; and bake in a strong heat.

Captains.—Rub four ounces of butter into seven pounds of flour; wet up with a quart of water; break your dough smooth; and bake in a good strong heat.

Drop.—Warm your pan; then put in one pound of powdered loaf sugar and eight eggs; beat it with a whisk till it becomes milk-warm; then beat it till it is cold; stir in a pound of sugar, two ounces of fine sifted flour, with about half an ounce of caraway seeds; put your batter into the bladder, and drop it through the pipe, in quantities about the size of a nutmeg, on wafer-paper; sift sugar over the top, and bake in a quick oven.

Filbert.—Rub a pound of butter into three pounds and a half of flour; make a hole, and put in ten ounces of powdered loaf sugar; wet up with four table-spoonsful of honey water, one of orange-flower water, and three-quarters of a pint of milk; break your dough smooth; mould them as large as a nutmeg, and as round as you can; cut them twice across the top each way, about half through, with a sharp knife; place them on your tin; and bake them in a steady heat.

Lemon.—Prepare your dough as for filbert biscuits, only leave out the orange-flower water, and use about six drops of the essence of lemon; cut them out, and dock them with a lemon docker; bake them in a good steady heat.

Naples.—Take six ounces of good moist sugar, and six ounces of loaf; a quarter of a pint of water; and proceed the same as for diet cake, with six eggs, and three-quarters of a pound of flour; have your tins papered; fill them nearly full of the batter; sugar over the tops; and bake them in rather a brisk oven. These biscuits are, in fact, nothing more than diet-bread batter, fancifully dropped into tin, papered with white paper, and baked in a warm oven, with a little sugar sifted over the top.

Queens.—Rub one pound of butter into two pounds of flour; mix one pound of powdered sugar with it; then make a hole and pour in a quarter of a pint of milk, to mix it up with; you may add a few caraways, if you choose; roll the paste in sheets of the thickness of a halfpenny; cut them with an oval to about the size of an egg; place them on clean tins, but see that they do not quite touch, prick them with a fork, and bake them in a slow oven till they begin to change colour; when they are cold, they will be crisp.

Rout.—Powder one pound of loaf sugar, and soak it in three parts of half a pint of milk; let it stand two hours; then add two table-spoonsful of honey water, and one egg; rub half a pound of butter into two pounds of flour; make a hole in it, and mix it up with your sugar and milk. Or you may rub half a pound of butter into two pounds of flour, make a hole and put one pound of powdered sugar in the middle; then pour in three parts of half a pint of milk, and two table-spoonsful of honey water; mix it up together; let it lie ten minutes; cut it out, and place them in buttered tins, see they do not touch; wash with milk, and bake quickly.

Savoy.—Powder and sift one pound of loaf sugar; sift one pound of flour; warm a pan, and put in the sugar; break one pound of egg upon it; beat both together with a whisk till it becomes warm—beat till it is cold, and then stir in your flour; have a bladder and pipe ready; put your batter into the bladder, and force it through on sheets of paper; sift sugar over them and bake in a quick oven; when cold turn them up, and with a washing brush wet the bottom of the paper; turn them back again, and in five minutes they will come off easily.

Seedy.—Rub one pound of butter into seven pounds of flour; roll one pound of moist sugar fine, and put into the middle with two ounces of caraway seeds; wet up with one pint and a half of milk, and one pint of honey water; bake in a hot oven.

Wine.—Take two pounds of flour, two pounds of butter, and four ounces of sifted loaf sugar; rub the sugar and the butter into the flour, and make it into a stiff paste with milk; pound it in a mortar; roll it out thin, and cut it into sizes and shapes to your fancy; lay them on buttered paper, in a warm oven, or iron plates brushed with a little milk. When done, you can give them a glaze by brushing them over with a brush dipped in eggs. A few caraway seeds may be added if thought proper.

York.—Prepare your mixture as for filbert biscuits; dock them with the Duchess of York, or any other docker—they are best baked in a hot oven, and not washed over.

Powder.—Dry your biscuits in a slow oven; roll them and grind them with a rolling-pin on a clean board till the powder is fine; sift it through a fine hair-sieve, and it is fit for use.

Drops.—Take half a tea-cup of water, six eggs, and one pound of sifted loaf sugar—whisk them together till thick; then add a few caraway seeds, and eighteen ounces of flour—mix it lightly together, and drop the mixture on wafer-paper, about the size of a small walnut; sift sugar over them, and bake in a hot oven.

Cracknels.—Rub six ounces of butter into three pounds and a half of flour—make a hole, and put in six ounces of powdered loaf sugar—wet up with eight eggs and a quarter of a pint of water—break your dough smooth—make them and dock them like a captain's biscuit—form them on your reel; drop them into a stew-pan of water boiling over the fire—when they swim take them out with a skimmer, and put them into a pailful of cold water; let them remain full two hours before you bake them—you may drain them in a cloth or in a sieve—bake them on clean tins in a brisk oven, or on the bottom of the oven.

SECTION I.—THE OVEN.

Cakes.—Rich pound-cake; twelfth, or bride-cakes: butter two pounds twelve ounces, sugar one pound twelve ounces, currants five pounds, citron one pound and a-half, almonds six ounces, nutmegs, mace, and cinnamon, of equal parts, in powder, two ounces; eggs twenty, brandy half a pint—these proportions allow for the cake being iced. If more sugar is preferred, the quantity must be the same as the butter; but less is used in this instance, that the cake may be light, and also to allow for the fruit, which would make it too sweet. Double the quantity of almonds may be used if required, as some persons prefer more.

Warm a smooth pan, large enough for the mixture; put in the butter, and reduce it to a fine cream, by working it about the pan with your hand. In summer the pan need not be warmed, as it can be reduced to a cream without; but in the winter keep the mixture as warm as possible, without oiling the butter. Add the sugar and mix it well with the butter, until it becomes white and feels light in the hand. Break in two or three eggs at a time, and work the mixture well, before any more is added. Continue doing this until they are all used and it becomes light; then add the spirit, currants, peel, spice, and almonds, some or most of these being previously cut in thin slices, the peel having also been cut into small thin strips and bits. When these are incorporated, mix in the flour lightly: put it in a hoop with paper over the bottom and round the sides, and placed on a baking-plate. Large cakes require three or four pieces of stiff paper round the sides; and if the cake is very large, a pipe or funnel, made either of stiff paper or tin, and well buttered, should be put in the centre, and the mixture placed round it; this is to allow the middle of the cake to be well baked, otherwise the edge would be burnt two or three inches deep before it could be properly done. Place the tin plates containing the cake on another, the surface of which is

covered an inch or two thick with sawdust or fine ashes to protect
the bottom. Bake it in an oven at a moderate heat. The time required to bake it will depend on the state of the oven and the size of
the cake. When the cake is cold, proceed to ice it. (See Icings for
Cakes.) Wedding-cakes have generally, first, a coating on the top
of almond icing ; when this is dry, the sides and top are covered
with royal or white icing. Fix on any gum paste or other ornaments whilst it is wet; and when dry, ornament it with piping,
orange-blossoms, ribbon, &c. ; the surface and sides are often covered
with small knobs of white sugar candy whilst the icing is wet.

Twelfth-cakes are iced with white or coloured icing, and deco
rated with gum paste, plaster ornaments, piping-paste, rings, knots,
and fancy papers, &c., and piped.

Savoy Cakes (hot mixture).—One pound of loaf sugar powdered,
one pint of good eggs, and fourteen ounces of flour. Warm a pan,
free from grease, with the sugar in it in the oven until you can
scarcely bear your hand against it ; then take it out and pour in the
eggs : whisk the whole together with a birch or wire whisk until it
is quite light and cold, when it will be white and thick. If it should
not whisk up well, warm it again and beat it as before ; or it may be
beat over the stove fire until it is of the warmth of new milk. When
it is finished, sift the flour and stir it in lightly with a spoon, adding
a few drops of essence of lemon to flavour it. Butter some tin or
copper moulds regularly, so that there is not more on one place than
another, nor too thick either, with rather less on the top of the mould
than the sides. Dust it with loaf sugar sifted through a lawn sieve.
Knock out all that does not adhere, and again dust it with fine flour ;
turn it out, and knock the mould on the board as before. Tie or pin
a piece of buttered paper round the mould, so as to come two or three
inches above the bottom. Fix the mould in a stand and nearly fill it.
Bake in a moderate oven. When done, the top should be firm and
dry. Try it by pushing in a small piece of stick or whisk, and if it
comes out dry, it is done. The surface of the cake should be quite
smooth. There is as much art in buttering the mould properly as in
preparing the mixture, if not more.

Cold Mixtures.—Separate the yolks from the whites when you
break the eggs. Put the yolks into a clean pan with the sugar, and
the whites in another by themselves. Let the pans be quite free
from grease. If they are rubbed round with a little flour, it will
take off any which may be left about them. Wipe them out with a
clean cloth. Beat up the yolks and sugar by themselves, with a
wooden spoon, and afterwards whip up the whites to a very strong
froth. If they should happen to be rather weak, a bit of powdered
alum may be added. When the whites are whisked up firm, stir in
the yolks and sugar. Sift the flour and mix it in lightly with the
spatula, adding a little essence of lemon to flavour it. Fill the
moulds and bake as before. When cakes are made in this way, the

eggs should be quite fresh and good, otherwise the whites cannot be whipped up. When weak, pickled eggs are used. I find a good method is to beat the eggs first by themselves, over a fire, until they are warm; then add the sugar, and whip it over the fire until it is again warm, or make as for hot mixtures, and heat it twice.

Almond Savoy Cakes and Almond Hearts.—One pound of blanched sweet almonds (four ounces of them may be bitter), two pounds of sugar, one pint of the yolks of eggs, half a pint of whole eggs, one pound of flour, and the whites of twelve eggs beat to a firm froth.

Pound the almonds with the sugar in a mortar, and sift them through a wire sieve, or grind them in a mill, and mix them with the sugar in the mortar. First mix the whole eggs well with the almonds and sugar, then add the yolks by degrees, stirring the whole until quite light; then mix in the whites, and afterwards the flour, lightly; prepare some moulds as for Savoy cakes; but some only butter them. Fill the moulds three parts full and bake them in a moderate oven. For almond hearts, butter some tins in the shape of a heart, but without bottoms; cover a baking-plate with paper; place the tins on it, and fill them nearly three parts full with the mixture: dust a little sugar on the top, and bake them in a moderate oven.

Venice Cake.—Take a Savoy cake and cut it in slices, half or three-quarters of an inch thick, in a parallel direction from the bottom to the top; spread over each slice with raspberry or apricot jam, or some of each alternately, or any other sort of preserve. Replace each piece in its original form; when completed, make an icing as directed for cakes, with four whites of the eggs to a pound of sugar, which will make it rather thin. It may be coloured with cochineal, &c.; spread it over the cake, which, being thin, will run into the flutes and mouldings of the cake, when it will appear of the same form as before. Let it dry in the mouth of the oven, but be careful it does not get discoloured. When it is dry, ornament it with piping. Savoy cakes are often done in the same manner, without being cut in slices, to ornament them; or they may be done without icing, and either piped or ornamented with gum paste borders, &c., which are fixed on with dissolved gum Arabic. Volutes or high and projecting figures are supported with small wire.

Savoy Cake to represent a Melon.—Bake a cake in a melon-mould; when cold, cover it with icing as for a Venice cake. Whilst it is wet, stick on some pieces of loaf sugar, to imitate the surface of the melon. Strew over it some yellow and green sugar-sands; or paint it when dry to imitate nature. Form the stalk, leaves, &c., out of gum-paste, and fix them in the centre, on the top.

Savoy Cake to imitate a Hedgehog.—Bake a cake in a mould of that form; blanch some Valentia or Jordan almonds; cut them into small fillets and stick them over the surface, to form the quills or prickles of the hog. Put in two currants for the eyes.

10

Bordeaux or Parisian Cakes.—Make a mixture as for pound-cakes leaving out the fruit, peel, spices, &c.; bake it in a round or oval hoop. When baked and cold, cut it into slices, half an inch thick; spread each slice over with jam or marmalade. The outside of the cake may be cut round, or fluted to form a star; and the centre of the cake is occasionally cut out to about an inch and a half from the edge, leaving the bottom slice whole: this may be filled with preserved wet or dry fruits, creams, or a trifle. The top is ornamented with piping, wet or dry fruits, and peels, or piped with jam and icing.

Italian Bread.—One pound of butter, one pound of powdered loaf sugar, one pound two ounces of flour, twelve eggs, half a pound of citron, and lemon-peel. Mix as for pound-cake. If the mixture begins to curdle, which it is most likely to do from the quantity of eggs, add a little of the flour. When the eggs are all used, and it is light, stir in the remainder of the flour lightly. Bake it in long, narrow tins, either papered or buttered: first put in a layer of the mixture, and cover it with the peel cut in large thin slices; proceed in this way until it is three parts full, and bake it in a moderate oven.

Rice Pound-Cake.—One pound of butter, one pound of powdered loaf sugar, twelve ounces of flour, half a pound of ground rice, and twelve eggs. Mix as Italian bread, and bake it in a papered hoop. If it is required with fruit, put two pounds of currants, three-quarters of a pound of peel, one nutmeg, grated, and a little pounded mace.

Wafers.—Four ounces of sugar, four ounces of butter, eight ounces of flour, the yolk or white of one egg, and half a tea-cupful of milk or water. Melt the butter in the water; mix the egg, sugar and flour together, adding, by degrees, the melted butter and water; or, instead of the butter, it may be made into a thin batter with cream, and a little orange-flower water, or any other essence, to flavour it. The mixture may be coloured. Make the wafer-tongs hot over the hole of a stove or clear fire. Rub the inside surfaces with butter or oil, put in a spoonful of the batter, and close the tongs immediately; put them on the fire, turning them occasionally until the wafer is done, which a little practice will soon enable you to ascertain; roll the wafers on a small round stick, stand them on their ends in a sieve, and put them in the stove to dry; serve them with ices.

CAKES.

Almond Cakes.—Take one pound of sweet Valentia, or Province almonds—cover them with boiling water in a saucepan; let them just boil up, then strain them out of the water, and rub them out of their skins; cut about two ounces of them into thin slices; put the rest into a mortar, with one pound and a half of loaf sugar, the whites of six eggs, and one table-spoonful of orange-flower water; pound it fine; lay your wafer-paper on the tin, and drop your almond cakes on it about the size of a walnut—then drop a few of your cut almonds on each of them, and bake them in a slow oven.

Almond Savoy.—Take one ounce of bitter and three ounces of sweet almonds; boil and skin them; put them into a mortar, with the yolks of six eggs, and half a pound of loaf sugar, pounded very fine; then whisk up the whites of the eggs to a strong froth, and mix it as lightly as you can with the rest; then stir in four ounces of flour as lightly as you can; bake it in a slow oven, if in a hoop you must paper it, and sugar your cake over the top; but if in a shape, you must butter the shape; then shake fine sugar over into it before you put in the batter.

Bride. — Wash and pick one pound and a half of currants very clean; dry them in a cloth—stone four ounces of Muscatel raisins— add a quarter of an ounce of mace, and half as much cinnamon; pound it fine in a mortar; boil four ounces of Jordan almonds in a little water; strain the water off, skin them and pound them fine; take two ounces of citron, two ounces of candied orange, and two ounces of candied lemon peel; cut them into thin slices; break eight good new eggs into a basin; take one pound and a quarter of fine flour, and sift in one pound of loaf sugar powdered fine; warm a pan, and beat one pound of best butter with your hand, till it comes to a very fine cream; put in your sugar, and beat it together till it is fine and white —then put in a fifth part of your flour; give it a stir, and put in nearly half your eggs; continue to beat it; add a little more flour, and the rest of your eggs; beat it again; stir in the rest of your flour and currants — then add your almonds, raisins, candied peel, spice, and half a gill of the best brandy—mix all well together; paper your hoop with double paper round the side and bottom; put in your cake, and bake in a very slow oven.

Bath.—Take one pound and a quarter of good moist sugar; roll it fine—put in a pan with three-quarters of a pint of water; let it stand all night; rub three ounces of butter into four pounds and a half of flour; make a hole and pour in your sugar with half a pint of honey water—rub it out thin—cut out, and place them on buttered tins— wash with water, and bake in a quick oven.

Banbury.—Take one pound and a half of flour, and one pound of butter; roll your butter and part of the flour out in sheets; wet up the rest of your flour with one or two table-spoonsful of good yeast, and about a quarter of a pint of water; roll out your paste in a large sheet; double it up and roll it out again; do the same five times; cut it up in square pieces, not more than one ounce and a half—have a few currants mixed with a little candied peel chopped fine, a little moist sugar, and a little brandy—put two tea-spoonsful on each piece; bring the two corners together over the middle, and close them up in an oval shape; turn the closings downwards; shake a little powdered sugar over the tops—put them on a cold tin; let them stand awhile in the cold to prove them, and bake them in a steady oven.

There is another method, which is as follows :—

Take two pounds of currants, half an ounce each of ground allspice and powdered cinnamon; four ounces each of candied orange and lemon peel; eight ounces of butter, one pound of moist sugar, and twelve ounces of flour; mix the whole well together; roll out a piece of puff paste; cut it into oval shapes; put a small quantity of your composition into each, and double them up in the shape of a puff; put the whole on a board, flatten them down with a rolling-pin, and sift powdered sugar over them—do not put them too close together; bake them on iron plates in a hot oven.

Breakfast. — Put a tea-spoonful of good yeast into two pounds of flour; mix the yeast and a little of your flour with a half pint of warm milk, about the consistence of batter. When your paste has risen well, take a little milk,—melt three ounces of butter in it; put a tea-spoonful of salt, and the yolks of eight eggs into the flour and yeast, and with the milk and butter mix it well into dough. Be careful that neither your butter nor milk is so hot as to scald the flour or yeast, and also that your dough is not too soft. Make your paste into cakes about two inches thick; put them into buttered hoops: lay the hoops on iron plates, and when they are lightly risen, bake them in a warm oven. When done, cut them into slices half an inch thick, and butter each slice as you would a roll; then cut them into pieces, and serve up for breakfast or tea.

Cinnamon, Currant, and Caraway.—Rub one pound of butter into three pounds and a half of flour; make a hole, and put in one pound of powdered loaf sugar; then wet it up with half a pint of honey water, and half a pint of milk. Divide your dough into three parts; add to one part a little powdered cinnamon; to another a few currants: to the other a few caraway seeds. Roll them in sheets to the thickness of the currants; cut them about the size of a penny-piece; wash with a little milk, and bake in a good steady heat.

Common Cheese.—Take four ounces of butter; heat it with a wooden spoon in a warm pan, till it comes to a fine cream. Then add four ounces of powdered sugar; beat it well; add the yolk of one egg, beat again—then add one whole egg; beat all well together, and mix in four ounces of clean currants. Lay your puff paste in the patties; fill them half full; shake a little sugar over, and bake them in a good heat.

Curd Cheese.—Warm one pint of new milk; stir in a bit of rennet; keep it warm till a nice curd appears; break it to pieces, and strain the whey through a hair-sieve. Then, having your mixture prepared as for common cheese-cakes, but without any currants, put it into the sieve with the curd, and rub it all through together. Then mix in your currants; fill them out, and bake them in a good heat.

Almond Cheese.—Take three or four bitter, and one ounce of sweet almonds; boil and skin them; put them into a mortar, with two ounces of loaf sugar, and the yolks of two eggs; pound them fine. Then rub two ounces of butter to a cream, and mix all together. Put puff paste in the patties; fill them three-parts full with the batter; lay a few cut almonds over the top; sugar over, and bake them in a steady oven.

Lemon Cheese.—Prepare your mixture as for common cheese-cakes, and grate the rind of a nice fresh lemon, and mix with it. The currants may be left out or not.

Derby.—Rub one pound of butter in two pounds and a half of flour; make a hole, and put in one pound of powdered loaf sugar; beat two eggs with three table-spoonsful of honey water, and as much milk as will make up half a pint. Add half a pound of currants; mix all up together; make them what size you please, and bake them in a steady oven.

Diet Bread.—Whisk the yolks of twelve and the whites of six eggs together, so as just to break them. Put a quarter of a pint of water into a saucepan, or small stew-pan; add a pound of loaf sugar, and put it on the fire. Take it off just before it boils; put in the eggs, and stir it well together till cold; then stir in lightly one pound of flour, and put your mixture into square tins prepared. Sift sugar over the tops, and bake in a warm oven, till they are dry and firm on the tops. A few currants or caraway seeds may be occasionally used to vary them.

Ginger.—Prepare your dough as for Bath cakes, but add as much ground ginger as will give them a pleasant taste; cut them about the thickness of a shilling, and full as large as a penny-piece; wash them with water, and bake quick.

Lord Mayors.—Put one pound of sifted loaf sugar and eight eggs into an earthen pan; whisk them well for about five minutes, until quite thick. Then add a few caraway seeds, and a pound of flour; mix it all up lightly with a spoon, and drop them on paper, about the size of a small tea-cup; place them on iron plates; sift sugar or caraway seeds on the top, and bake in a hot oven. When done, take them off the papers, and stick two together.

Lunch, or School.—Rub half a pound of moist sugar into two pounds of flour; make a hole in the middle of it, and put in a table-spoonful of good thick yeast (not bitter); warm half a pint of milk rather more than blood-warm, but not hot enough to scald the yeast; mix it with the yeast and a little of the flour, about one-third part. When it has risen, which will be in about three quarters of an hour, if the yeast is good, melt half a pound of butter in a little more milk;—be careful it is not hot enough to scald the yeast. Add on pound and a-half of currants, a little candied peel, and grated rind of lemon, and a tea-spoonful of powdered allspice,—mix all together; butter your hoop, or tin, put it in, and set it in a warm place to rise. When it has risen, bake it in a warm oven. When you think it is done, stick in a small twig of your whisk, and if it comes out dry it is done; but if it is sticky, it is not sufficiently baked. The cake should be mixed up rather softer than bread dough. A few yolks of eggs mixed up with it will make it eat much better.

Moss.—Rub a little root cake paste through a fine sieve, and it will look like moss. Gently squeeze a little together, about the size of half-a-crown, and bake them on wafer paper of a light colour. After they are done, touch the tops with cochineal. If they are made up round, the finger pressed in the middle, and two or three caraway comfits put in, they will resemble birds' nests, with eggs in them; and to make the resemblance more complete, just touch the tops with a green colour.

Macaroon.—Prepare your mixture as for almond cakes (but do not cut your almonds), and add two spoonfuls of orange-flower water; lay them out on the wafer-paper, in an oval shape; sift sugar over them, and bake them in rather a brisk oven; when lightly coloured over, they are done.

Plum.—Set a sponge with one pound of flour, half a pint of warm milk, and about three table-spoonfuls of good yeast. Then take four ounces of butter, four ounces of powdered sugar, two eggs, and four ounces of flour. Proceed to beat it up the same as for pound cake; then put in your sponge, and beat all well together; after which, add one pound of currants, nicely cleaned. Paper your hoop to put it in; bake it without proving, and in a slow oven.

Pound.—Take one pound of butter, beat it with your hand in a warm pan till it comes to a fine cream; put in one pound of powdered loaf sugar—beat it together to a nice cream. Previously, have one pound and a quarter of flour, sifted; put in a little, and give it a stir; put in four eggs, and well beat it; then take a little more flour, and four more eggs, as before, and beat it well again; then stir in the remainder of your flour. If you bake them in small cakes, butter your tins; if in large cakes, paper your tins. Sugar over the top, and bake them in a moderate heat. Some persons use this method:— Sift one pound of loaf sugar, and add to it one pound of fresh butter, melted a little, and worked with the hand to the consistency of cream; beat them together, and while doing so, add ten eggs; keep beating the whole till well incorporated. Take four ounces of candied orange or lemon peel, shred or cut small, a few currants, and one pound of flour; mix the whole well together, and put in a hoop; sift some sugar on the top, and then bake in a warm oven.

Prussian.—Rub four ounces of butter into seven pounds of flour; wet up with one quart of milk, warm, one pint of warm water, four yolks of eggs, and half a pint of good thick yeast; but if you are obliged to take more yeast, leave out some of the water, or you will make them too poor: let your dough lie about ten or twenty minutes; mould them up round, about half or three quarters of a pound each; place them on your tins, about two inches from each other, and put them in a warm place, and prove them well. Bake in a good steady heat, and melt a little butter to wash them with when they are done.

Queens.—Melt one pound of butter a little, in a preserving pan, and then work it with the hands to the thickness of cream; put to it one pound of fine loaf sugar, well sifted, and beat it up for a minute or two; add eight eggs, and two spoonfuls of water; beat it up for two minutes, and add twenty ounces of flour, and a handful of currants; mix it well together; put them in small round tins, bake them in a hot oven, and in about five minutes give the tins a smart tap, and the cakes will fall out.

Queen's Drops.—Prepare your mixture the same as for pound-cakes, but add about two ounces more of flour, one pound and a-half of currants; drop them on whited-brown paper, in drops about the size of a large nutmeg, about two inches from each other; put your sheets on tins, and bake them in a steady oven.

Rout.—Take one pound of sweet almonds, boil them and skin them; then take one pound of loaf sugar,—pound both in a mortar, and get as much as you can through a sieve; put the rest into a mortar again, with four yolks of eggs, and the rind of a nice lemon; pound it very fine, and put in what has passed through your sieve, and mix it all together; cut them in blocks, or make them in any shape you please. Sprinkle them lightly with a little water; sift sugar over them, and put them on tins that have been rubbed with a bit of butter. See that they have room, so as not to touch each other; bake them in a rather brisk oven till they are lightly coloured over. If you see them coloured too deep at the bottom, put cold tins over them.

Raspberry.—To one pound of raspberry jam put one pound of loaf sugar, powdered, and sifted fine; mix it well together, and have a ring made of tin, with a handle on the side of it, about the size of a penny-piece; place the ring on a sheet of paper; fill it with the jam, and move your ring, and the cake will remain; do the same till the whole is done. Make the tops smooth with your knife as you fill them; then put them in a warm place to dry, till they get a little set; then take the crooked end of the handle of a spoon, and make five or six marks on the top of each cake. Set them to dry again, till they are fit to be removed; then take them off with the point of a knife; have a box prepared to put them in, and lay slips of paper between every layer of cakes.

Ratafias.—Take four ounces of bitter, and four ounces of sweet almonds—boil and skim them; put them into a mortar, with one pound of loaf sugar, and the whites of four eggs; pound it together very fine, and drop them out upon white-brown paper. See that they are all about the size of a nutmeg, and full an inch apart; shake sifted sugar over them, and bake them in tins, in a slow oven: when they are all of a colour they are done; when cold they will come off the paper.

Savoy. — Take care that the shape in which it is to be baked is clean and dry; butter it, and sift sugar into it, but turn out all the sugar that does not stick to the butter; then have half a pound of sifted sugar, and six ounces of sifted flour; warm your pan, put in your sugar, break in four whole eggs, and then one yolk; whisk it till it is first warm, and then cold; then stir in your flour, and turn your butter into the shape, and bake it in a slow oven; it will take about one hour. When done, turn it out bottom uppermost:—it will look very handsome for the middle of the table.

Sponge. — To three-quarters of a pound of powdered sugar, break three-quarters of a pound of eggs into a warm pan—whisk it till it is cold, and stir in half a pound of flour—have your tins ready buttered and sugared; put about three parts of a table-spoonful into each of them, sift sugar over them, and bake them in a brisk oven.

Seed.—Proceed as directed for pound-cakes, but instead of currants and candied lemon-peel, substitute a few caraway seeds — omit the sugar on the top.

Shrewsbury.—Powder three-quarters of a pound of loaf sugar, and mix it with one pound and a quarter of flour—chop three-quarters of butter into pieces amongst it, with the scraper—then add one white and three yolks of eggs — mix it together to a smooth paste; roll it into thin sheets, and cut out your cakes about the size of half a crown —place them on clean tins not to touch—bake them in a slow oven till they begin to change colour.

Tea.—Beat eight eggs into a pan with a whisk till they come to a good head—then add one pound of loaf sugar powdered—beat both together till it becomes thick and whitish—then stir in one pound of sifted flour, but do not beat it again—take a spoon in your left hand and a knife in your other—lay a sheet of paper on your tin; take up a spoonful of batter, and with your knife strike as much out of the spoon as will make a cake the size you like—see that they are about an inch apart, and make them as round as you can — bake them in a rather brisk oven till they are nicely coloured over; if they do not come off the paper easily, when cold, damp the bottom as directed in Savoy biscuits. You may vary these cakes by dropping caraway seeds, sugar, or currants, on the top, before you bake them.

Twelfth.—Prepare your mixture as for pound-cake, plum-cake, or bride-cake, which you please—if you prepare it for pound-cake, take two pounds of currants, four ounces of candied orange and lemon peel, to every pound of sugar—make them of any size you please—when done, ice them over, as directed in page 104, and lay on your ornaments while the icing is wet. You may get the ornaments from the wholesale confectioners.

Yorkshire.—Rub four ounces of butter into seven pounds of flour, wet up with one quart of warm milk, one pint of warm water, and half or three-quarters of a pint of good yeast, let it prove about twenty minutes, make it into cakes and put them on warm tins—see that they have room so as not to touch—when well proved, make a hole in the middle, the size of a large thimble—bake them in a hot oven—when done, wash them with a little melted butter.

York Drops.—Bruise eight ounces of sweet almonds in a mortar, having bleached and dried them as directed—add the whites of three eggs, and rub them with the pestle till quite fine—then add the whites of four more eggs, and one pound of sifted loaf sugar—mix all well together, and lay it out on paper the size of large peas; bake in a warm oven, or on iron plates, and when done and cold, take them off the paper.

[*Anne Page's.*—One pound of butter, two pounds of flour, one pound of the best loaf sugar, two ounces of caraway seed, half a pint of good rose-water. Rub the sugar into the butter, and then mix carefully in the sifted flour and caraway seed with the rose-water. Roll the mass thus formed into sheets to about the thickness of a dollar, and shape with small tin cutter; lay them on baking-dishes, and bake in a moderate oven.

These are commonly called A. P.'s.

York Cakes.—Rub into six ounces of butter one pound of sifted flour; then mix together half a pound of pulverized loaf sugar, four ounces currants, well washed and dried, and half an ounce of powdered cloves; rub in with the butter and flour half a pint of warm milk; roll out the paste into thin sheets, and cut with a round cutter, and bake at a moderate heat.

Jumbles.—Half a pound of butter, half a pound of the best loaf sugar, pulverized, half a pound of finely-sifted flour; rub intimately together with three eggs and half a wineglass of rose-water, add half an ounce of ground cinnamon and one grated nutmeg; bake in a moderate heat on waxed tins.

Cinnamon Biscuit.—Grind in a clean mortar a quarter of a pound of sweet almonds, blanched; to which add, gradually, the whites of three eggs, and then three-quarters of a pound of the best pulverized loaf sugar, and two ounces of ground cinnamon; form into a paste, which should be laid out on greased tins, in diamond or other shapes; ice with cold water, to produce a gloss, and bake.

Hazlenut Kisses.—Beat one pound of pulverized white sugar with the whites of eight eggs over a slow fire until they are light, then add four ounces of blanched filberts, cut fine; lay them out on paper, and bake in a slow oven.

Vanilla Biscuit.—Beat with a whisk the whites of ten eggs to a very strong froth, add three-quarters of a pound of finely-pulverized loaf sugar, ten ounces of sifted flour, three cloves of vanilla pulverized with three ounces of loaf sugar. Stir all these ingredients together for one minute, and put the batter into paper bag or cornet; lay out on waxed tins, and bake in a moderate oven.

Trifle.— Place several alternate layers of Savoy biscuit and bitter almond maccaroons in a handsome glass bowl, or dish, and saturate them with the best Madeira wine; cover the surface of the top layer with any kind of jelly, jam, or marmalade (red currant jelly is generally preferred); then take the whites of four eggs, half a pound of pulverized loaf sugar, the juice of one sound lemon, a little rose-water, and one pint of cream; whisk all to a froth, and put lightly into the bowl, in the shape of a cone; and ornament according to fancy, with coloured sugars.

Cocoanut Cakes.—One pound of blanched sweet almonds, the whites of twelve eggs, three pounds of the best pulverized loaf sugar, three large cocoanuts, finely grated.

Pound the almonds in a clean mortar, with the whites of the twelve eggs, until the mixture is perfectly smooth, then add the pulverized sugar and the grated cocoanut, and work the whole in the mortar into a tolerably stiff paste; form the cakes about the size of a walnut, and lay out on baking-plates previously well waxed.

Sans Soucies.—One pound of blanched sweet almonds, the whites of three eggs, two pounds of pulverized loaf sugar.

Pound the almonds with the whites of the eggs until reduced to a smooth paste, and then gradually mix in the sugar. Roll a portion of the mass thus formed in powdered sugar, and cut them into pieces about an inch long, and form them into the letter S, and bake on wax plates.

Cocoa Biscuit. — Three-quarters of a pound of blanched sweet almonds, half an ounce of good Caracas cocoa, previously roasted, two eggs, three pounds of pulverized loaf sugar.

Incorporate in a clean mortar the almonds, cocoa, and the eggs, until the mass becomes perfectly smooth, then add the sugar, with a small portion of vanilla, in powder. Form the biscuit with a tin cutter of fancy shape; lay on waxed plates, glaze the surface of the cakes with cold water, and bake in a tolerably quick oven.

Lady Cake.—Two pounds of powdered loaf sugar, half a pound of fresh butter, seven ounces of blanched sweet almonds, and one ounce of blanched bitter almonds.

Beat in a clean mortar the almonds till reduced to a smooth paste, adding occasionally a little rose-water, to prevent them from oiling; add the sugar and butter; then add the whites of thirty fresh eggs, previously whisked to a very strong froth; then mix in, very lightly, two pounds of finely-sifted flour, and bake in tin pans about twelve inches long, eight broad, and two inches deep. This cake requires a quick oven — thirty to thirty-five minutes will be sufficient time. When cool, ice as before directed, and score with a sharp knife.

Lady Fingers.—Put the yolks of four eggs in a small basin with four ounces of pounded sugar, on which you have grated the peel of one good fresh lemon; work this well with a spatula for five minutes;

after which ceat up the whites of the four eggs, and when they are very stiff, pour a fourth part of them on the yolks, which you afterwards mix with the remainder of the whites, with the addition of two ounces of sifted flour, stirring continually, to make the whole very smooth.

Then form your biscuits on half sheets of white paper, folded in such a manner that they are only three inches in length, and no larger than your finger. As soon as one sheet is full, cover your biscuits with fine sugar, and place on a baking-plate, which you put in the oven as soon as the surface of the biscuits become glossy by the melting of the sugar. Bake in a moderate oven, and when they have acquired a fine colour take them out ; when sufficiently cool, remove from the paper by moistening the opposite side, or with the blade of a very thin knife. Place them afterwards two and two, with their backs to each other, in order not to injure the glossy sides.

Biscuit à la Cuillière (Spoon Biscuit).—Mix the yolks of three eggs with four ounces of fine sugar and half a clove of vanilla, powdered and passed through a silk sieve; after working these ingredients for five minutes, add a whole egg, then work them again for five minutes; after which add another whole egg, and continue to work them for five minutes longer ; then beat up the whites of the first three eggs to a very stiff froth, and mix them, together with two ounces of dried and finely-sifted flour, to the former ingredients: when the batter is quite sleek, lay out on paper, and bake as Lady-fingers.

Small Biscuits with Almonds.—Prepare three yolks as usual ; work them ten minutes with four ounces of sugar and an ounce of pounded bitter almonds ; add a whole egg, and work together full five minutes longer ; then beat up the whites very stiff, and mix them with the yolks, together with one ounce and a half of wheat flour dried in the oven and passed through a fine sieve: work this batter till it is quite sleek, and then pour it in small copper moulds formed like small melons, carefully buttered and covered twice with sugar. Mask the biscuit with fine sugar, and bake in a moderate oven.

Biscuits with Cream. —After mixing the yolks of three eggs with four ounces of fine sugar, (on which half the peel of a small lemon has been grated), work the mixture for ten minutes; then beat up the three whites as usual ; mix them gradually with the yolks, together with one ounce and a half of dried sifted flour, and four spoonsful of whipped cream, well drained: the whole being lightly mixed together and very sleek, put it in moulds or cases, covering the tops of the biscuits with fine sugar ; when the sugar is melted, put the biscuits in a gentle oven, and let them bake twenty or twenty-five minutes. When taken out of the oven, be careful to put them on their sides to prevent their sinking.

Biscuits glazed with Chocolate.—Prepare the same ingredients as the last, but flavour them with half a clove of vanilla pounded and passed through a silk sieve; then put them in a case ten inches in

.ength by seven in width, which you put in a gentle oven In forty
or fifty minutes after, see if your biscuit feels tolerably firm , if it does,
take it out of the oven, and as soon as it is quite cold, turn the case
and take out the biscuit, which you cut into small squares, lozenges,
&c.: then mix the white of an egg with an ounce of finely-powdered
white sugar and three ounces of chocolate, which, after being grated,
you have dissolved for a few minutes in the mouth of the oven: work
the whole with a silver spoon for five minutes, adding a little white
of egg to make it rather thick and glossy, and then cover the top of
the biscuit thickly with it, smoothing it with a spatula ; after which
put the biscuit for five or six minutes in the oven, and then let cool.

Biscuits glazed with Orange.—Rub the peel of a fine orange on a
piece of sugar, then scrape off all the coloured parts, and, after bruis
ing them with a rolling-pin, mix them with three ounces of fine sugar
and the white of an egg ; beat the whole for five or six minutes, then
glaze the biscuit (prepared like the last, except you omit the vanilla)
with it.   Flavour the biscuit with either the half of an orange peel,
lemon or citron, or with coffee.   If you wish to glaze them *à la rose*,
colour the glazing with vegetable red, and add one drop of essence
of roses to it.]

FANCY BREAD, GINGER-BREAD, BUNS, ROLLS, MUFFINS, CRUMPETS, &C.

Almond Bread.—Having bleached and dried eight ounces of sweet,
and once ounce of bitter almonds, bruise them in a mortar; add one
egg, and with the pestle rub it all very fine.   If you find it getting
oily before it becomes fine, increase the quantity of egg.   When fine,
grate into it the rind of one lemon; and add one pound two ounces of
sifted loaf sugar.   Mix with yolks of eggs, until it becomes a soft
batter ; now add to the rest two ounces of flour, and mix all well together ; then pour your batter into square flat buttered tins, with the
sides and ends turned up about two inches high; bake in a warm
oven, and when cold, ice it over with the icing (see article to ice,
bride, and other cakes, p. 104), and sprinkle some nonpariel sugar-
plums on the top.   You may cut it in any shape or form, and mix
it with your rout cakes.

Colchester.—Prepare your dough as for Bath cakes; cut it with a
Colchester cutter to about the thickness of a penny-piece, wash it
with milk, bake it quick, wash it with egg and milk, while hot; when
baked and cold, cut them apart.

Diet.—Put three-quarters of a pound of loaf sugar into a saucepan,
with a quarter of a pint of water; put it over a steady fire and stir it
till it is dissolved ; beat six eggs with a whisk in a pan; when the
sugar boils, pour it gently on the eggs, keeping it well beat till cold;
then stir into it three-quarters of a pound of fine sifted flour ; have

your frames papered, fill them three parts full with the batter, sift sugar over them, and bake them in a steady oven.

French Rolls.—Set a sponge with a quart of warm water, and half or three-quarters of a pint of good yeast; let your sponge rise and drop, then melt one ounce of butter in a pint of warm milk, and one ounce of salt, to wet up with; it will take about seven pounds of flour altogether; let it lie about half an hour, then put them on warm tins; prove them well, and bake them in a quick oven.

Short Bread.—Rub one pound of butter into three pounds of flour; make a hole and put in one pound of powdered sugar ; then wet up with a quarter of a pint of honey water, a quarter of a pint of milk, and two eggs; break them in round pieces about as big as a walnut; roll them round or oval, to the size of a tea-saucer ; pinch round the edge; place them at the distance of one inch from each other on clean tins, not buttered ; cut half a pound of candied orange or lemon peel into pieces, and lay them on the top of your cakes; bake them in a good steady oven.

Queen's Ginger-Bread.—Take two pounds of honey, one pound and three-quarters of the best moist sugar, three pounds of flour, half a pound of sweet almonds blanched and cut thin, half a pound of candied orange; peel the rinds of two lemons, grated, and an ounce of powdered cinnamon, half an ounce of nutmeg, cloves, mace, and cardimoms, mixed and powdered, and a wine-glassful of water; put your honey and water into a pan over the fire, and make it quite hot ; mix the other ingredients into the flour, and pour in your honey, sugar, and water, and mix all well together; let it stand till next day : make it into cakes and bake it; rub a little clarified sugar until it will blow in bubbles through a skimmer, and with a paste-brush rub over your ginger-bread when baked.

Spice Ginger-Bread. — Take three pounds of flour, one pound of moist sugar, four ounces of candied lemon or orange peel, cut small, one ounce of powdered ginger, two ounces of powdered allspice, half an ounce of powdered cinnamon, a handful of caraway seeds, and three pounds of treacle ; rub the butter with your hand into the flour; then add the other ingredients, and mix it in the dough with the treacle ; make it into cakes or nuts, and bake them in a warm oven.

Thick Ginger-Bread.—Prepare seven pounds of treacle, rub three-quarters of a pound of butter into twelve pounds of flour; mix three ounces of caraway, two ounces of ground coriander seeds, and two ounces of ground allspice, with your flour and treacle ; mould it well together, make it into cakes, point them, butter the sides, and place them close together on buttered tins; put up-sets round them, wash with milk, and bake in a steady heat; when they are done, wash with egg and milk.

Sweetmeat Nuts.—Prepare seven pounds of treacle ; mix four ounces of ground ginger, six ounces of ground allspice, eight ounces of can died lemon and orange, cut small, with nine pounds of flour; wet it up with your treacle, then beat into your dough four pounds of butter, and five pounds of good moist sugar; lay them off on buttered tins, about the size of walnuts, flat them down, wash them with water, and bake them in a slow oven.

Spice Nuts.—Prepare seven pounds of treacle; rub half a pound of butter into nine pounds of flour; mix four ounces of ground allspice, four ounces of ground ginger, two ounces each of caraway and coriander seeds powdered with your butter, flour, and treacle; roll half a pound of moist sugar, and strew it over the top, so that you take a little in every piece you cut from it; roll them out in long rolls about the size of your finger; cut them in pieces the size of a nutmeg; place them on buttered tins, but not to touch; wash with water or small beer, and bake in a good steady oven.

Muffins.—Muffins are baked on a hot iron plate, and not in an oven. To a quarter of a peck of flour add three-quarters of a pint of yeast, four ounces of salt, and as much water (or milk) slightly warmed, as is sufficient to form a dough of rather a soft consistency. Small portions of the dough are then put into holes, previously made in a layer of flour about two inches thick, placed on a board, and the whole is covered up in a blanket, and suffered to stand near a fire, to cause the dough to rise; when this is effected, they will each exhibit a semi-globular shape; they are then placed on a heated iron plate, and baked; when the bottoms of the muffins begin to acquire a brownish colour, they are turned, and baked on the opposite side.

[*Wheat Muffins.*—Melt a small piece of butter into a quart of milk, and set it aside until cold — beat four eggs very light, and make a batter by adding alternately and very gradually a little milk and a little flour, until the batter is of the proper consistence, which is quite thin — then add a large spoonful of yeast, if you do not use the powders as directed in the note on page 123. Bake them in muffin-rings on a griddle, and butter them before serving, — they must be torn asunder to butter, as cutting them open renders them heavy.

Rice Muffins.—Rice muffins are made in the same manner exactly as rice cakes, except that the batter of the former is thinner—that is, to a quart of milk and three eggs, you put less rice and less flour.

Rice Cakes.—Boil half a pint of rice until quite soft, setting it aside until perfectly cool; beat three eggs very light and put them with a pint of wheat flour to the rice, making it into a batter with a quart of milk; beat it well, and set it to rise with a spoonful of yeast, or use the yeast powders as directed above. Bake on a griddle, and butter them before sending them to table.

Buckwheat Cakes.—To a quart of buckwheat meal put a little Indian meal (say a table-spoonful) and a little salt; make them into a batter with cold water, taking care to beat it *very* well, as the excellence of buckwheat cakes depends very much on their being well beaten:

then put in a large spoonful of good yeast,* and set to rise; when sufficiently risen, bake them a clear brown on a griddle. They are usually buttered before being sent to table.

Flannel Cakes.—Melt a table-spoonful of butter in a quart of milk, and after stirring it well, set it away to cool; then beat four eggs very light, and stir them into the milk in turn with half a pound of sifted flour; put in a spoonful of yeast, and set it aside. These are baked on a griddle like buckwheat cakes, and are always buttered before being sent to table.

Indian Slappers.—To a pint of Indian meal, add a handful of wheat flour and a little salt; beat three eggs very light and stir them, in turn with the meal, into a quart of milk. These cakes require no yeast, and should be baked as soon as mixed. They are baked on a griddle, and buttered before serving.

Johnny-Cake.—To a quart of sifted Indian meal (for this cake coarse meal should always be used) add a pint of warm water, and a tea-spoonful of salt; mix the meal gradually into the water, and when mixed beat it very hard, until quite light, then spread it out smoothly and evenly upon a board. Let this board be then placed before the fire, having something to support it behind; when done, cut it in squares, and send it to table, without butter.

Corn-Meal Bread.—To a pint of sifted corn-meal (not too fine) add a small piece of butter and two eggs, well beaten; make it into a batter with new milk, and put in a spoonful of yeast. It will require an hour to rise. This bread is best baked, in small tin pans.]

Crumpets.—Crumpets are made of batter composed of flour, water (or milk), and a small quantity of yeast. To one pound of the best wheaten flour you may add three table-spoonfuls of yeast. A portion of the liquid paste, not too thin (after being suffered to rise), is poured on the heated iron plate, and baked, like pancakes in a pan.

Rusks.—Rub six ounces of butter into four pounds of flour; set a sponge with a pint and a-half of warm milk, and a half pint of yeast; when the sponge rises, add four ounces of good moist sugar, mix it up together, let it prove a little, then roll it out about the size of a rolling-pin; flat it down with your hand, and place the cakes at a

---

* Many persons now make use of the yeast powders, and give them a decided preference. They certainly possess the advantage of requiring less time, and thereby enabling you to make muffins, buckwheat cakes, &c.—which, set with yeast, require some hours in the preparation—at a quarter of an hour's notice. The ingredients are the super-carbonate of soda and tartaric acid, to be used in the following manner:— A spoonful of soda, and a spoon *two-thirds* full of tartaric acid, are to be dissolved *separately* in a little water. The soda is to be put into the batter when it is partly beaten, taking care that it is *perfectly* dissolved; and the acid is to be added when the cook is *ready* to begin baking, as they must not be allowed to stand after the effervescence takes place.

aistance from each other, so as not to touch; prove them well, and bake them in a moderately heated oven; when cold, cut them in slices; place them to touch on the tins, and brown them off in a brisk oven.

Sweet Rusks.—Cut a diet bread cake into thin long slices; lay them on iron plates and brown them quickly, in a very hot oven; turn them when of a light-brown colour; and when of a similar colour on the other side, they are done.

Tops and Bottoms.—Prepare your mixture as for rusks, make it into small balls about the size of a large walnut, place them on your tins in straight rows just to touch; prove them well; bake them in a moderate heat: when cold, draw a sharp knife between every row; to cut your balls out square, turn them on their side, and cut them through the middle one at a time: place them on the tin as close as you can, with the cut part upwards; put them in a brisk oven; watch them till they are nicely browned over; then they are done.

OF PASTES IN GENERAL—PRELIMINARY REMARKS.

[The first grand object for our consideration is the proper method of *making paste;* for upon our skill in that important branch of the pastry-cook's art, will the success of our future operations mainly depend. Whenever the paste happens to be ill made, its bad effects will invariably appear in the baking; and if even by chance the colour should turn out tolerably well, it will be still highly unsatisfactory to competent judges; in short, paste thus made will always be heavy, have an unpleasant flavour, and, above all, be very indigestible; and, indeed, it is owing to the general ignorance that prevails respecting its proper amalgamation, that good pastry is so rarely made; and that the number of good family pastry-cooks is so small.

It is much more easy to *bake* pastry than to make it. The oven requires care, constant attention, and practice, it is true; but the art of making pastry is quite another thing—an art that admits of no mediocrity—a good memory, taste practice, and dexterity, being absolutely necessary in that branch of the business; for it is really from the manner of mixing the various ingredients of which it is composed that it acquires its good or bad quality.

An indispensable requisite is cleanliness in those who have to prepare elegant viands, and the most scrupulous attention must be paid to delicate management and order. In a pastry-cook these requisitions are absolutely indispensable.

TO MAKE PUFF PASTE.

I shall now endeavour to give directions for the composition of this delicate and elegant kind of paste.

Ingredients.—Twelve ounces of fine-sifted flour, twelve ounces of butter, two drachms of fine salt, and the yolks of two eggs.

Manner of Working.—Having placed the twelve ounces of flour on the board, make a small hole in the middle ; in which, put the two drachms of salt, the yolks of two eggs, and nearly a glass of water ; and with the ends of the fingers of your right-hand gradually mix in the surrounding flour, adding a little water where necessary, till the paste is of a proper consistence, rather firm than otherwise ; then prove it by leaning your hand on the board, and working it for some minutes, when the paste will become soft to the touch, and glossy in appearance.

It is of importance to observe, that this paste should be neither too stiff nor too soft, but of a proper medium ; yet it will be better when it is a little too soft than when too stiff.

The same process must be attended to in summer as in winter ; though many persons pretend that this kind of paste should be made stiffer in summer than in winter, on account of the difference in the two seasons. As far as regards the hardness of the butter, this mode of reasoning has certainly some truth in it ; for, inasmuch as the winter is favourable to the work, so does the heat of summer render our operations troublesome and difficult, and prevent them sometimes from having the desired effect, particularly in the making of puff paste.

The reason why summer paste should not be made softer than that made in winter, is this :—if, when the paste is soft, it be buttered, and afterwards placed on ice, as is practised in summer, the butter, which is a greasy substance, will become quickly congealed by the coldness of the ice ; while the paste, which is only a moist body, will scarcely be affected by it ; and, consequently, the butter being frozen, and the paste soft, it will follow that, in working it, the butter not being held by the paste sufficiently firm to unite with it, will break into small pieces ; and after having received the two first turns, will appear in small lumps, like large peas. On rolling it again, and placing on the ice, the cold acts with greater force on the small particles of butter, which quickly become like so many icicles, and the paste, in consequence, will be completely spoiled ; for, in baking, these particles of butter melt, and, separating themselves from the paste, render it incapable of uniting with them.

When the paste has been made as above, take three-quarters of a pound of butter, in pieces, which for twenty minutes has been in a pail of spring water, thoroughly imbued with a few pounds of pounded ice previously well washed ; then squeeze and work well in a napkin in order to separate the water from it, and at the same time to render it soft, and above all, of an equal consistence ; then as quickly as possible roll the paste on a marble slab, into a square, and placing the butter in the middle, cover with an equal thickness of paste, by raising the paste over it. After rolling it out two or three feet in length, fold it into three parts by doubling one part over the other; after which roll it out again, and fold it once more into three equal parts—now roll it to a greater length, envelope it with a clean linen cloth which has been dusted with some sifted flour—lay this on some finely pounded ice, taking care to have several folds of cloth between the paste and the ice, to prevent the moisture striking through—place on the top of the paste a dish containing some pounded ice—this serves to keep the surface of the paste cool, and also to prevent it becoming soft by the action of the air. After three or four minutes, remove the dish, and turn the paste upside down, instantly covering it a before. This operation should be performed three times in the same manner, and with the same precautions.

Lastly, roll it out two or three times according to what you intend to make of it, and use it as expeditiously as possible, lest the heat of the season should render it too soft to handle, or prevent its having the desired effect in baking.

Thus, in less than half an hour, it is possible to make very fine puff paste, having previously everything ready—the ice pounded, the butter frozen, and the oven quite hot, otherwise it cannot be done. This is important, as it is sometimes an hour before the oven can be made hot ; and therefore the paste should not be begun to be made till the oven is half heated. The following is another method.]

Puff Paste.—Take one pound of flour, and one pound of good firm butter; cut your butter into slices; roll it in thin sheets on some of your flour; wet up the rest with about a quarter of a pint of water; see that it is about as stiff as your batter; roll it to a thin sheet; cover it with your sheets of butter; double it in a three double; do the same five times; then double it up; lay it in the cold to use when you want it, keeping the air from it : you ought to make it before the sun rises, unless you have a cold place to make it in. The following is another method : — Take one pound of flour, and eight ounces of butter; rub the butter into the flour with your hand, and make it into a paste with water, to the consistence of very thick batter; roll out your paste thin; break eight ounces more butter into pieces of the size of a shilling, and put them in all parts of your paste; fold it up ; and after standing a short time, roll it out again; when it has been rolled out three times, it is fit for use.

Short Paste.—Rub one pound of butter into one pound and a quarter of flour; wet it up stiff with cold water; work it smooth, and it i fit for use.

Tart Paste.—Eight ounces of butter rubbbed into a pound of flour with your hand, and made into a stiff paste with water, is an excellent paste for tarts.

Apricot Tart.—Lay your puff paste in patties; put your jam in the middle, and bake them in a brisk oven; or you may bake your puff paste first with a bit of bread in the middle; then take out the brea —fill the hole with jam; it will look very handsome.

Covered Tart.—Take your short paste; cut it into pieces to the size of your patties; roll them out thin; lay in the bottoms; put your fruit as high as you can; put a pinch of sugar on the top; close your tart; sprinkle water over it; put a pinch of powdered loaf sugar on the top; and bake them in a good steady heat.

Raspberry Tart.—Take your short paste; cut it into pieces of nearly the size of your patties; about the thickness of a penny-piece; then with your thumb drive it thin in the middle; leave it thick at the edge; cut it round close to the patty, and notch it with the back of your knife; thin your raspberry-jam with a little water, and fill the tart three parts full; bake them in a brisk oven. Or you may made them with puff paste, in the same manner as apricot tarts, if you choose.

Mince Pies.—Stew three pounds of lean beef till it is tender; chop it fine with one pound and a half of beef suet, one dozen of apples, and one pound of stoned raisins; mix all together, with three pounds of currants, washed and picked clean, half a pound of citron, half an ounce, together, of cloves, cinnamon, and mace, pounded fine, a little allspice, a pint of brandy, and three half pints of cider, and one pound and a half of good moist sugar; squeeze it close down in a glazed pan, and it will be fit for use; then roll your puff paste in sheets, about the thickness of a penny-piece; cut out the tops to the size of your pies; put your cuttings for bottoms; fill them to your fancy; cover and close them; and bake them in a steady oven.

Raised Pie.—Take seven pounds of flour; then take one pound of mutton suet, clarified down; put it into a saucepan with one pint and a half of water, and set it over the fire till it boils; make a hole in the middle of your flour, and pour in your liquor boiling hot; then mix in your flour with a spoon till you can bear to put your hand in; mix it till it becomes a nice smooth piece of dough; cover it over with a cloth; and raise your pies with as much of it as will make the size you want; when filled and nicely closed, wash with egg, and lay on your ornament. Your oven must be brisk, if for small pies; but if for large ones, a more steady heat will be best.

THE BAKER.

INTRODUCTION.

BAKING, or the art of making bread, is amongst the earliest modes resorted to by the more advanced portions of mankind for the preparation of food. In the early ages, however, loaf or leavened bread was unknown, as it is amongst uncivilized nations to this day. The North American Indians contrive, by pounding their maize, or Indian corn, to make a sort of cake, which they bake by means of hot cinders. This serves them, and, indeed, occasionally the Anglo-Americans, as a substitute for loaf or leavened bread, and may be called unleavened bread. But in some parts of the world bread is not known; in others it may be known, but is not used—as amongst the people inhabiting the vast Pampas on the Rio de la Plata, where scarcely anything is eaten but beef.

Bread may be thus defined ;—A nutritive substance made of corn, generally wheat, or other farinaceous or mealy vegetables, ground or reduced into flour or meal, that is, a powder more or less fine, and kneaded or mixed with water, and baked in an oven, upon hot ashes or other grise. This process makes unleavened bread, or, in other words, unfermented bread, or what is now called biscuits. To leavened or fermented bread, that is, the bread generally used in our houses, there must be an addition, yeast, or some other substance which has the property of promoting fermentation.

The origin or etymology of the word bread is not without interest. Horne Tooke says, bread is *brayed* grain, from the verb to bray or pound in a mortar, the ancient way in which flour was made. The meaning of bread, therefore, is something brayed—brayed wheat, or wheat bread — pease brayed, or bread — oats brayed, or bread, &c. The word bread was spelt differently in different ages; thus we have *brede*, breed, &c. Dough, Horne Tooke says, comes from the Anglo-Saxon word *deaw-ian,* to wet, to moisten. *Dough*, or *dow*, means wetted. The bread, that is, brayed corn or grain, by being wetted becomes *dough*.

Loaf comes from the Anglo-Saxon word *hlif-ian*, to raise, to lift **up.**

Thus, after the bread or brayed corn has been wetted, by which it becomes dough, then follows the *leaven*, by which it becomes *loaf*, that is, *raised*. Leaven is derived from the French word *lever* to raise.

Bread, in some countries, is not made entirely of meal, much less of wheaten flour. In many parts of Sweden, the bread is composed partly of the bark of trees, particularly during winter.

In Westphalia, a kind of very coarse black bread is made, of which the peasants bake one large loaf for the whole week. This is divided for use with a saw. It is called pumpernickel, and is sometimes exported. In many parts of Germany, bread is made of grain nearly entire, or but just bruised, which is very coarse, and frequently forms part of the food of horses.

The Romans, before they had acquired the art of baking, were called, either by way of distinction or reproach, the pulse-eating people. According to some authorities, indeed, the earlier nations knew no other use of their meal than to make of it a kind of porridge. Such was the food of the Roman soldiers for several centuries, or at most their skill extended no farther than to knead unleavened dough into cakes or biscuits. Even at present, as has been before intimated, there are many countries where the luxury of bread is unknown.

Loaf-bread is seldom used in the northern parts of Europe and Asia, except by the higher classes of inhabitants. You never see loaves in Sweden, though in the towns rolls are common enough. Gottenburg is a considerable town, containing between twenty and thirty thousand inhabitants. In the year 1812 it was crowded with merchants from all parts of Europe, being at that time the great connecting link between Great Britain and the Continent. Towards the end of that year only, the captain of an English packet ordered a Gottenburg baker to bake for him a quantity of bread, amounting altogether to the value of one pound sterling. The baker was astonished, and in fact confounded, at so great an order, and refused to comply till the captain gave him security that he would carry off and pay for the loaves, declaring that he could never dispose of so great a quantity of bread in Gottenburg, if it were left on his hands. In the country parts of Sweden, nothing in the character of bread is to be met with, excepting rye cakes, which are represented as nearly as hard as flint, and which are only baked twice a year.

GENERAL REMARKS ON BAKING.

Baking, as a business or profession, was never confined to the baking of common bread alone, that is to say, bread in every-day use. A baker we take to mean a person who bakes and prepares any farinaceous substance intended for human food. If this definition be correct, then it will follow that not only loaf-bread baking, biscuit-baking, fancy-bread baking, belong to the business of the baker, but also pas-

21

try making and confectionery. We know, indeed, that all these branches are frequently to a certain extent practised by the same individual, and therefore, in a work of this kind, they ought all to be treated of, which we intend to do under separate heads.

The ancients had a great variety of spice bread and sweetmeats, and these, there is every reason to believe, were produced by the persons called bakers; pastry-cooks and confectioners being unknown as separate professions. The Asiatics were exceedingly fond of sweetmeats, and there can be little or no doubt that a similar taste was introduced by them among the Romans, when they were carried to Rome to practise their calling there. The Rhodians, we are told, had a particular kind of bread sweetened with honey, so exquisitely pleasant, that it was eaten with other delicacies after dinner by way of dessert.

The French, who are excellent bakers, have a great variety of breads, and these for the most part have been long introduced into Great Britain. The common bread of that country, or bread for general use, may be divided into three classes:—wheaten bread, made of the finest flour, sometimes called firsts; second, or household bread, made of flour somewhat coarser, called seconds; and brown bread, made of flour called thirds, and sometimes of flour of various degrees coarser than thirds. The coarseness or fineness of flour (supposing the wheat of the same quality) depends upon the dressing, or the separating of the flour from the husks of the wheat, after it has been reduced to a powder. The finest flour is entirely separated from the bran or husks—the other description not entirely so, but the broad bran is removed from the coarsest flour. The writers in many of our celebrated Encyclopædias say, that "our household bread is made of the whole substance of the grain, without the separation of either the finest flour or the coarsest bran." This is a mistake altogether.

In making pure wheaten loaf bread, no other ingredients should be employed but flour, water, yeast, or some other innocent fermenting matter. Various other ingredients are used, principally by those engaged in making bread for sale. The London bakers employ alum, for the purpose of making the bread whiter, &c. Home-baked bread is never so white, even when made from the same flour, as that produced by the public baker; but of this we shall speak when we come to describe the methods of bread-making used by public bakers; at present we shall confine ourselves to bread as made in families for daily use.

The goodness of bread, whether baked at home or abroad, will depend, firstly, upon the quality of the flour employed; secondly, upon the quality of the yeast; and, thirdly, upon the skill and care of the baker. The process of baking, though simple enough, requires some experience on the part of him or her who may undertake to perform it. We need scarcely say, that experience is only to be acquired in one way, and that way is too obvious to need pointing out. To judge of flour, experience is also necessary; but any one may form a pretty accurate idea whether it is good or bad, by attending to the following directions:—If flour is of a fine white colour, it may be pronounced good, so far as colour is concerned; but if it be brown, it shows that either it was made from bad wheat, or that it has been coarsely dressed—that is, particles of bran, more or less fine, have been left in it. Brown flour, however, may be of a good, sound quality, and fine white flour not so. To judge of flour, take a portion in your hand and press it firmly between your thumb and fore-finger, at the same time rubbing it gently, for the purpose of making a level surface upon the flour. By this means you will be able to ascertain the colour, by observing the pressed and smooth surface; and the act of pressing and smoothing it, will enable you to ascertain these facts. If it feel loose and lively in the hand, it is of good quality; if on the contrary it feels dead or damp, or in other words clammy, it is decidedly bad.

Flour ought to be a few weeks old before it is used; but it will keep good much longer, if kept in a dry place covered over. But it is, perhaps, better to trust to your miller or mealman, who, if you are a good and constant customer, will take care to serve you with good flour for his own sake; for if he employs any tricks, he is sure to be discovered when the bread comes out of the oven.

It has been found by analysis, that wheat flour consists of three principal substances, namely, starch, gluten, and sugar, and a very small portion of albumen; of these, the starch is the most nourishing as food. The gluten resembles animal glue in its tenacious qualities; and its smell, when subjected to a strong heat, is fœtid, like burning horn or feathers. It will not ferment in warm water and yeast, but like a piece of flesh will become putrid. Mr. Edlin says, that " this substance is totally different from vegetable matter, but rather resembling animal." The gluten in wheat-flour is the cause of its forming an adhesive paste with water, and of its rising in leaven.

Starch forms the most considerable part of wheat-flour, and there is reason to believe, from so many persons subsisting on potatoes, which contain much starch and no gluten, that it is the most nutritious; but starch cannot be made into bread, because it wants the mucilaginous gluten to give it tenacity, and the saccharine matter, or sugar, to induce fermentation.

From experiments made by Mr. Edlin, it appears that a pound of wheat contains three ounces of bran, ten ounces of starch, six drachms of gluten, and two drachms of sugar; which, with the loss of two ounces in grinding and reducing the flour to starch, make one pound, or sixteen ounces. From this it appears that he did not discover the albumen, which M. Seguin considers the fermenting principle.

Mr. Edlin also ascertained by experiment, that starch, isinglass, and sugar, mixed in proper quantities, and fermented with yeast, will make a light and porous bread.

Flour-paste may be considered as merely a viscid and elastic tissue, the interstices of which are filled with starch, albumen, and sugar.   We know that it is from the gluten that the dough derives its property of rising on the admixture of leaven ; the leaven acting on the sweet principle of the wheat, gives rise in succession to the vinous and acetous fermentation, and of consequence to alcohol, acetic, and carbonic acids.   The latter gas tends to fly off, but the gluten resists its disengagement, expands like a membrane—forms a multitude of little cavities, which give lightness and sponginess to the bread.

To judge of good yeast, no positive directions can be given.   Yeast should always be fresh, and if made from table ale it is better, because less bitter than that made from very strong ale.   If the yeast is sour, the dough will not rise.   Originally what is called leaven was uniformly employed, and it is now sometimes used as a substitute for yeast.   Those who use it, keep a pound or more dough from baking to baking.   It is kept in a wooden barrel, or bowl, covered with flour. Before it is fit to use, it must be both stale and sour.   Bread made in this way is said to be more digestible, but it is not so pleasant to the taste.   Leaven is now only used at sea.

A good oven is necessary for the production of good bread.   If the oven be heated, as in country places, by dry wood, furze, or fern, burnt in the oven itself, it ought to be built round, not long, as there will be in the former case a greater equality of heat.   The roof should be from twenty inches to two feet high in the centre; the mouth no larger than will be sufficient to admit the bread.   But many people who make their own bread send it to be baked at the baker's. We have seen good ovens attached to a stove, and heated by the kitchen fire.   These are not sufficiently capacious to contain loaves enough for the consumption of a large family, but they answer the purpose of a small family very well.   To save room, it will be necessary, in stove ovens, to bake in tins.   Bread thus baked is much more smooth and neat than when baked in the ordinary way ; but the pleasant crispness of the crust is wanting.

The ovens used in London and some other large towns are, for the most part, heated by a furnace placed on one side.   The heat in these ovens is very equable, and the baker is enabled to keep it up at all times with very little trouble, and with less expense than by the old method.

FAMILY LOAF-BREAD.

Under this head we shall give directions for making bread of wheat flour only.   The manufacturing of barley flour, rye flour, and a mixture of different kinds of flours, with or without the addition of various other nutritive substances, &c., into bread, will be treated of hereafter.

Family or Home-Baked Bread.—An expeditious and simple method of making bread for a small family is as follows:—Take half a bushel of flour; put all this flour excepting about four pounds into a tub or pan, and in winter place it before the fire to warm. Mix six ounces or half a pound of powdered salt with the flour—but it would be better to work the salt in with the dough. Then take a pint of good fresh yeast, and well mix it with a sufficient quantity of blood-warm water. Make a deep hole in the middle of the flour;—pour the water and yeast gradually into the hole of the flour, mixing the water and flour with your hands till both become well incorporated. Cover this mixture up, and place it near the fire till it has well risen, that is to say, fermented. Then work the other flour into it with your fists, till it becomes a nice, smooth, tough dough. Make this dough into loaves, and bake in an oven properly heated: if too hot, your bread will be burnt outside, and not done inside. It will take from an hour and a half to two hours in baking, but the bread should always remain in the oven half an hour after it has become brown; or, as it is technically called, it will not be soaked through. This is a method we have known to be used with success in many families, though not aware that it ever has been published before.

For large bakings, the following method is best:—

The common way is to put the flour into a trough, tub, or pan, sufficiently large to permit its swelling to three times the size it at present occupies. Make a deep hole in the middle of the flour. For half a bushel of flour take a pint of thick fresh yeast—that is, yeast not frothy—mix it with about a pint of soft water made blood-warm. The water must not be hot. Then gently mix with the yeast and water as much flour as will bring it to the consistence of a thick or stiff batter—pour this mixture into the hole in the flour, and cover it by sprinkling it over with flour—lay over it a flannel or sack, and in cold weather place it near, not too near, the fire. This is called laying the sponge. When the sponge—or this mixture of water, yeast, and flour—has risen enough to crack the dry flour by which it was covered, sprinkle over the top six ounces of salt—(more or less to suit the taste): mind, the time when the salt is applied is of great importance. We have seen directions in which we are told to mix the salt with the water and yeast. The effect of this would be to prevent fermentation, or, in other words, to prevent the sponge from rising. After the salt is sprinkled over the sponge, work it with the rest of the flour, and add from time to time warm water (not hot) till the whole is sufficiently moistened; that is, scarcely as moist as pie-crust. The degree of moistness, however, which the mixture ought to possess can only be taught by experience—when the water is mixed with the composition, then work it well by pushing your fists into it—then rolling it out with your hands—folding it up again—kneading it again with your fists, till it is completely mixed, and formed into a stiff, tough, smooth substance, which is called dough—great care must be taken, that your dough be not too moist on the one hand, and on the other that every particle of flour be thoroughly incorporated. Form your dough into a lump like a large dumpling, again cover it up, and keep it warm to rise or ferment. After it has been rising about twenty minutes, or half an hour, make the dough into loaves, first having shaken a little flour over the board to prevent sticking. The loaves may be made up in tin moulds, or if it be desired to make it into loaves to be baked without the use of moulds, divide the dough into equal parts, according to the size you wish to have your loaves—make each part into the form of a dumpling, and lay one dumpling, if we may so speak, upon another—then, the oven being properly heated, by means of an instrument called a peel, a sort of wooden shovel, put in your loaves, and immediately shut the door as close as possible. A good deal of nicety is required in properly placing the loaves in the oven—they must be put pretty closely together. The bread will take from an hour and a-half to two hours to bake properly.

Brown or *Diet Bread* is made of flour from which the coarsest flake bran only is removed. This bread is made as in the preceding directions. By boiling a pound and a-quarter of bran in a gallon of the water in which the bread is made, and then straining it, there will be an increase of one-sixth more than if mixed with plain water.

Bread not liable to become bitter.—This process is an invention of a Mr. Stone. He took a tea-spoonful of yeast and mixed it with three quarters of a pint of warm water. He then took a bushel or fifty-six pounds of flour, and having put it into the kneading trough, and made a hole in the middle of it large enough to contain two gallons of water, he poured in his small quantity, and took a stick and stirred it until it was as thick as a batter pudding—having covered this sponge with a sprinkling of flour, it was left to ferment for an hour, at the end of which time he took a quart more of warm water and poured in, and repeated the operation of stirring it in with more flour, and again sprinkling it with flour, when it was again left for two hours, when it will be found to have risen and broken through the flour—then add three quarts or a gallon of water, and stir in flour to the consistence of butter, and again cover it with dry flour—and in about three or four more he mixed up his dough; which done, he covered it up warm and let it stand to prove four or five hours more, when he made up his loaves and baked them. The bread was as light and as porous as if one pint of yeast had been made.

Having, as we trust, explained the process of baking as it is practised by those who adhere to its simple principles, and who employ no other ingredients than those necessary to produce good bread, we shall now proceed to describe the methods pursued by the public baker; and, at the same time, give a description of a public bake-house, and the duties of the persons employed therein.

ARTIFICIAL YEASTS.

Previous to entering upon the subject of public baking, by which so large a portion of the people are supplied with their daily bread, it will be necessary to lay before our readers some of the various methods by which yeast is compounded. Of brewers' yeast, or the yeast of ale and beer, we have already spoken, and therefore it will be necessary again to revert to it. Several of the following directions for the preparations of yeast have been long before the public, and some of them the writer has not had an opportunity of testing by experience, but there is no reason to doubt of their efficiency; of the patent yeast, however, now pretty generally used by the public bakers, he can speak with confidence, having witnessed the whole process of making it, and experienced its perfect applicability to the manufacturing of bread. We shall first, however, treat of the mode of preserving brewers' yeast.

Yeast to Preserve.—Take a quantity and work it well with a whisk, till it becomes thin; then procure a wooden dish or platter, clean and dry, and with a soft brush lay a thin layer of yeast on the dish, and turn the top downwards to keep out the dust, but not the air, which is to dry it. When the first coat is dry, lay on another, and let that dry, and so continue till the quantity is sufficient; by this means, it may soon be made two or three inches thick, when it may be preserved perfectly good, in dry tin canisters, for a long time. When you use it for baking, cut a piece and lay it in warm water till it is dissolved, when it is fit for use.

Potatoe Yeast is made of mealy potatoes boiled thoroughly soft — they are then skinned and mashed as smooth as possible, when as much hot water should be put on them as will make a mash of the consistency of good beer yeast. Add to every pound of potatoes two ounces of treacle, and when just warm stir in for every pound of potatoes two large spoonsful of yeast. Keep it warm till it has done fermenting, and in twenty-four hours it will be fit for use. A pound of potatoes will make nearly a quart of yeast, and it is said to be equally as good as brewers' yeast.

The following are Dr. Lettsom's directions for making another Prepared Yeast.—Thicken two quarts of water with four ounces of flour, boil it for half an hour, then sweeten it with three of brown sugar; when almost cold, pour it along with four spoonfuls of bakers' yeast into an earthen jug, deep enough for the fermentation to go on without running over; place it a day near the fire; then pour off the thin liquor from the top, shake the remainder, and close it up for use, first straining it through a sieve. To preserve it sweet, set it in a cool cellar, or hang it some depth in a well. Always keep some of this yeast to make the next quantity that is wanted.

Artificial Yeast.—Take two ounces of flour, boil it in a quart of water, till it comes to the consistence of a thin jelly, pour it into a machine for impregnating water with fixed air; then put into the lower vessel some coarse powdered marble, and pour on it some sulphuric acid diluted with water. The apparatus is now to be adjusted, and the upper vessel put in its place, and nearly stopped. The fixed air now passes through the valve, and ascends into the middle and upper part of the machine, where the gas is absorbed by the flour jelly in considerable quantity; and in the course of a few hours the matter will be found so strongly impregnated, as to be in a state of fermentation. This artificial yeast may now be put into a bottle for use. The great advantage of this yeast is, that it may be made in situations where it is impossible to procure brewers' yeast. The foregoing operation need not be performed but once by the same individual, as the process may be carried on by mixing this *artificial yeast*, which was invented by the late Mr. Henry, with the preceding preparation recommended by Dr. Lettsom, which it will cause to ferment the same as brewers' yeast.

Another artificial yeast is made as follows:—Take half a pound of fine flour, the same quantity of coarse brown sugar, and a quarter of a peck of bruised malt; boil these over the fire for a quarter of an hour, in half a gallon of water, then strain the liquor through a sieve into an upright jug, and when cooled to 80 degrees of heat, add one pint of the artificial Seltzer water, or, if procurable, Seltzer water itself, or water impregnated with fixed air—the mixture will soon begin to ferment: it should then be set before the fire, and when ebullition ceases, the yeast will sink to the bottom. Pour off the clear liquor, and the yeast will be fit for use.

Patent Yeast, which is extensively used by the London bakers, and which is, perhaps, preferable to all other yeasts, is made as follows: —Take half a pound of hops and two pailfuls of water, mix and boil in the oven till the liquid is reduced to one pailful; strain the decoction into the seasoning tub, and when it is sufficiently cool put in half a peck of malt. In the mean time, put the hops, strained off, again into two pailfuls of water, and boil as before till they are reduced to one; strain the liquid while hot into the seasoning tub. The heat will not injuriously affect malt, previously mixed with tepid water. Boil the hops again as before, and strain off as before into the seasoning tub. When the liquor has cooled down to about blood-heat, strain off the malt, and add to the liquor two quarts of patent yeast set apart from the previous making. It ought to be observed, that brewers' yeast will not answer the purpose.* To the malt and hops some add a little flour, but the patent yeast is quite as good without the flour, which in summer is apt to make the yeast go sour. By the

* If this be the case, it may be fairly asked, by what means the first patent yeast was generated? The answer is, by a chemical process similar to that invented by Mr. Henry, and which we have given under the head of ARTIFICIAL YEAST.

above process five gallons of very good yeast may be made, which will be ready for use the day after it is made. It occupies in manu facturing from about seven o'clock in the morning till two or three in the afternoon ; but it gives very little trouble to the baker.

ALUM, POTATOES, &c.

These ingredients are now considered indispensable by the London bakers in the manufacturing of second or household bread, that is, the bread in daily use in the metropolis. The effects of alum upon bread are not well understood : but it is generally said to bleach and act as an astringent. Accum says, that " the theory of the bleaching property of alum, as manifested in the panification (making into bread) of an inferior kind of flour, is by no means well understood ; and indeed it is really surprising, that the effect should be produced by so small a quantity of that substance, two or three ounces of alum being sufficient for a sack of flour. From experiments in which I have been employed, with the assistance of skilful bakers, I am authorized to state, that without the addition of alum, it does not appear possible to make white, light, and porous bread, such as is used in this me-tropolis, unless the flour be of the very best quality."

Mr. A. Booth, the lecturer on Chemistry, asserts, that "alum bleaches from the attraction of alumina, one of its constituent parts, to the colouring matter of the flour, and also acts as an astringent on the bread."

If these opinions are to be relied upon, of course the question is settled, as to the indispensability of alum in making London bread. Accum asserts, that he, in conjunction with skilful bakers, has tested the thing by experiments, which prove that alum cannot be dispensed with. For our part, we are inclined to think, that the whiteness of the London bread is owing, in some degree, to the process of baking, a process widely differing from that followed by women in making oome-baked bread ; which, as we have elsewhere asserted, is never so white or so porous, though made of the same flour, as bakers' bread. Accum, whatever talent he might possess as a chemist, was a fraudu-lent writer, and therefore his assertions are not to be relied on, as to the experiments which he alleges he had made. We agree with him, however, in his observation, that "the theory of the bleaching property of alum, &c., is by no means well understood."

The quantity of alum used in baking is much less than the public generally imagine, even by the most fraudulent of cheap-bread bakers, and indeed much smaller than many of the bakers themselves ima-gine. This may appear a strange assertion, and it is probably one never made before in print ; but a little explanation will make the point quite clear. It is well known that the bakers are liable to a heavy fine if alum is found on their premises. To avoid this liability as much as possible, they have long been in the habit of buying the

alum ready powdered at the druggists, under the appellation of *stuff*.
The druggists keep this *stuff*, which the bakers imagine is unadul-
terated ground or powdered alum, but which is, in fact, a compound,
consisting of one part alum, and three parts of muriate of soda, that
is, common table salt.   This compound is made by pounding the salt
with the alum in a mortar, and is kept by the druggists in pound
packages, which they sell at twopence each.   For this statement we
have the authority of several druggists, and the evidence of our own
eyes.   It may appear extraordinary that the bakers should suffer
themselves to be so *cheated;* but be this as it may, we believe it to be
the fact.   It should be recollected, that few bakers are readers, particularly of scientific or medical works.   In the fourth edition of
Gray's supplement to the Pharmacopœia and Treatise on Pharma-
cology, under the head of *stuff*, this term is thus defined :—" Alum, in
small crystals, one pound, common salt three pounds, to mix with
flour for baking."   We have the evidence of our own senses for knowing, that the respectable bakers of home or household bread do not put
more than half a pound or eight ounces of *stuff* to a sack of flour ; and
this stuff, as we have shown on the authority of Gray, only contains
one-fourth part, or two ounces, of alum, the remainder being common
salt.   Some persons, however, will ask for powdered alum, but the
druggist, knowing from the quantity required and the appearance of
his customer that it is wanted for baking, uniformly serves him with
the before-described mixture of salt and alum.   This we have frequently seen done.   The object of the druggist is profit.   It would
be scarcely worth his while to sell powdered alum for twopence a
pound.   Gray, in his book, puts it down at one shilling and sixpence
a pound.   This is ridiculously too high to sell by the pound, but it is
generally charged a penny an ounce.   The writer, giving this infor-
mation to his baker, he exclaimed, " You don't say so!—the infamous
rogues—why the rascally druggists cheat us before we can cheat our
customers ! !"

Such being the case, it seems almost inconceivable, that so small
a quantity as two ounces of alum in two hundred and eighty pounds
of flour, the weight of a sack, should have any effect in bleaching it ;
especially when we consider that one hundred parts of alum contain
but a fraction more than ten parts of alumina, the only constituent in
alum, as we are informed, that possesses the property of bleaching.
Nevertheless, there can be no doubt that alum, though perhaps not
by itself, yet in conjunction with other ingredients, has the effect of
whitening the bread.   A circumstance occurred, which we have from
indisputable authority, of a baker leaving out of his dough, by acci-
dent, his usual quantity of *stuff*, containing not more than two ounces
of alum.   The consequence was a batch of brown bread, which he
was obliged to sell at half price.

Alum, it is true, is used in small quantities—for the most part in
quantities too small to affect the health, perhaps, materially ; but still,
as it only whitens the bread, and makes it otherwise more pleasing

to the eye, while it deteriorates its wholesomeness, and injures its flavour, one would suppose that the great majority of people would prefer home-baked bread, as it is called, or bread without alum. This, however, they do not do; and there is little probability that they ever will. The Londoners in particular do not like home-baked bread. There have been many instances of persons being induced for the sake of their health to eat it for a time, but they always return to the *alumed* bread; and we question whether there is a single baker in the metropolis who sells sufficient home-baked bread to support himself and his family.

Formerly every baker was his own mealman or miller. This is the case now in Glasgow, and in other parts of Scotland. The bakers buy their own wheat, and manufacture it into flour at their own mills, which are held by them as joint-stock proprietors.

It seems to be generally agreed, that alum in bread is detrimental to the health of those who consume it. The fact, however, is, that the bakers eat the same bread as their customers; and it appears very improbable, that there should be a set of men who knowingly poison themselves. The following is Dr. Ure's opinion upon the effects of alum eaten in bread:—

" The habitual and daily introduction of a portion of alum into the human stomach," says Dr. Ure, in his Dictionary of Chemistry, " however small, must be prejudicial to the exercise of its functions, and particularly to persons of a bilious and costive habit. And, besides, as the best sweet flour never stands in need of alum, the presence of this salt indicates an inferior and highly acescent food, which cannot fail to aggravate dyspepsia, and which may generate a calculus diathesis in the urinary organs."

To ascertain whether alum is present in bread, crumble a portion when somewhat stale into cold distilled water; then squeeze the mass through a piece of cloth, and pass the liquid through a paper filter. A limpid infusion will thus be obtained. A dilute solution of muriate of baryta, dropped into the filtered infusion, will indicate by a white cloud, more or less heavy, the presence and quantity of alum.

It is said, that to counteract the costive quality of alum, when consumed in large quantities, the bakers frequently use jalap in the composition of their bread. This we do not believe. Dr. Darwin says, that when much alum is used, it may be distinguished by the eye in the place where two loaves have stuck together in the oven: they break from each other with a much smoother surface than those which do not contain alum. We believe this to be correct;—indeed the bakers say, that this is one of their reasons for using alum.

When the statute was enacted by king John for regulating the price of bread, and during many of the subsequent statutes of assize, the baker was his own manufacturer, purchasing his own corn, and having it ground and separated into flour, pollard, and bran. According to Pownall s work on the assize of bread, which we have no

doubt is correct, this flour, or the flour from which the bran and pollard only are separated, was found, from an unvaried series of experiments made from age to age, through the course of many hundred
years, to be three-fourths in weight of the whole grain of wheat,
taking all sorts of wheats together; and the bread made from this
flour has always been decreed the standard of the food of bread corn.
But, by insensible degrees, the manufacture of bread became separated
into two distinct employments.   To this cause Mr. Edlin attributes
the custom — the pernicious custom, as he considers it — of making
bread from other flour than that we have described, which many persons assert is more wholesome and more nutritious than that made of
the finest flour.   The miller not considering himself liable to the
assize laws, made different kinds of flour, some of which was extremely fine and white.   The bread made of this flour was so very
white, and pleasing to the eye and palate, that in the course of a few
years it got into general use, and the people, particularly the Londoners, refused to buy the bread made of the whole of the grain,
except the husks, or coarse and fine bran.

To this circumstance, perhaps, may be attributed the almost universal use of alum in bakers' bread not made of the finest flour; and
very little of it is so made, for it is impossible from a second flour,
which is the flour generally used, to make bread white without the
employment of the bleaching properties of this ingredient.

The assize of bread has been for some time abolished, and the baker
is entitled to sell his bread for as much as anybody is willing to give
for it.   There is very properly still a heavy penalty attached to sell-
ing bread short of weight.

Potatoes, called by the bakers *fruit*, are used by them for the purpose of aiding the fermentation, and, as they say, for the purpose of
improving the appearance of the bread, and not for saving flour.
Indeed, in the small quantities in which we have seen them used, not
more than seven or eight pounds to two hundred and eighty pounds
of flour, there can be little or nothing gained by them.   Potatoes,
however, as well as damaged rice, are no doubt used in large quantities by cheap, fraudulent bakers.   We utterly disbelieve the stories
about bakers using ground bones to adulterate bread, for this reason—
namely, that the expense of making them fit for such a purpose would
be much greater than the cost of flour itself.

There are instances on record of convictions having been obtained
against bakers for using gypsum, chalk, and pipe-clay, in the manufacture of bread.

Carbonate of ammonia, which is sometimes used by bakers in pro
ducing light and porous bread from sour or damaged flour, does not
appear to be liable to the same objections as those urged against
alum; as the action of the former upon the bread is merely mechanical, no part of this salt remaining in bread after it is baked.   During
the operation of baking, it causes the dough to swell up into air bubbles, which carry before them stiff dough, and thus it renders the

dough porous; the salt itself is at the same time totally volatilized, and not a particle remains in the bread. Carbonate of ammonia, however, has not, like alum, the property of bleaching the bread.

It is said, that the carbonate of magnesia of the shops, when well mixed with flour in the proportion of twenty to forty grains to a pound of flour, materially improves it for the purpose of making bread. It is recommended to be employed when the flour is new, or of a bad quality. Mr. Davy, professor of Chemistry, says, that this substance must be most intimately mixed with the flour, previous to laying the sponge; and gives it as his decided opinion, that not the slightest danger can be apprehended from the use of so innocent a substance, in such small quantities as he recommends.

METHOD OF MAKING BAKERS' BREAD.

Having briefly described the utensils of a bakehouse, and having descanted at some length (but not longer, it is hoped, than the importance of the subject requires) upon the ingredients used by public bakers in the manufacture of bread, we shall proceed at once to show the methods they generally employ. We must observe, however, that the first method described was witnessed by Mr. Edlin nearly forty years ago; and the second, which is the mode now generally followed, has been witnessed by the writer himself in all its details.

The Old Method. — To make a sack of flour into bread, the baker bakes that quantity of flour, and empties it into the kneading trough —it is then carefully sifted through a wire sieve, which makes it lie lighter and reduces any lumps that may have been formed in it. The next process is to dissolve two ounces of alum, technically *stuff*, or some call it rocky, in a little water placed over the fire. This is then poured into the seasoning tub, and four or five pounds of salt are added to it, with a pailful of water pretty hot, but not too much so. When this mixture, technically *liquor*, has cooled to the temperature of about 84°, from three to four pints of yeast are mixed in it, and the whole having been strained through the seasoning sieve, is emptied into a hole made in the mass of the flour, and mixed up with a portion of it to the consistence of thick batter. Dry flour is then sprinkled over the top. This is called the *quarter sponge*, and the operation is denominated setting. The sponge must then be covered up with sacks or woollen cloths to keep it warm, if the weather be cold.

In this situation it is left three or four hours, when it gradually swells and breaks through the dry flour laid upon its surface. Another pailful of water, impregnated with alum and salt, is now added and well stirred in, and the mass sprinkled with flour and covered up as before. This is called setting *half sponge.*

The whole is then well kneaded, with about two pailsful of more water, for about an hour, when the dough is cut into pieces with a knife; and to prevent it spreading, pinned or kept at one end of the

trough by a pin board. In this state it is left to *prove*, as the bakers
call it, for about four hours. After the proving process is over, the
dough is again well kneaded for about half an hour. It is then
removed from the inside of the trough to its lid, where it is cut into
pieces, and weighed into the quanties suitable for each loaf.

The operation of moulding the dough can be learnt only by practice. It consists in cutting the masses of weighed dough, each into
two equal parts. They are then kneaded either round or long, and
one placed in a hollow made in the other; and the union is completed
by a turn of the knuckles on the centre of the upper piece. The
loaves are left in the oven from one hour and a half to two hours.
They are then taken out, and, to prevent their splitting, are turned
their bottom side upwards. They are afterwards covered up with a
blanket to prevent as much as possible evaporation, by which weight
is lost, and the bread becomes dry and unpalatable.

Mr. Edlin has made one mistake in the above account; namely, as
regards the time when the salt and alum are incorporated with the
flour. These ingredients ought never to be put into the sponge. If
they were, the salt would retard the fermentation, and this Mr. Accum
as a chemist ought to have known, and not, like many others, have
copied and adopted Mr. Edlin's error.

With the exception just alluded to, the foregoing mode of making
bread was pursued by the bakers some years ago, and is still practised
by some of them; but the following is the process now pursued.

Modern Method.—Take a peck of potatoes (about eight pounds) and
boil them with their skins on—then mash them in the seasoning tub,
add two or three quarts of water, about the same quantity of patent
yeast (as directed to be prepared, page 136), and three or four pounds
of flour; stir together well, and cover the mixture up close with a
sack, and let it stand from six to twelve hours, when it will have
become what is called ferment. Then empty a sack of second flour
into the trough—some sift it in—and take a little less than one quarter of the sack of flour, and pin or block it up to one end of the trough
with the pin-board. Then bring the seasoning tub with the *ferment*
in it to the trough, pour in a sufficient quantity of warm water — in
summer, cold — stir up the mixture with the hands, and mash any
lumps of potatoes (fruit) that may be in — next, strain it through a
sieve for the purpose of separating the skins of the potatoes, then
pour the mixture liquor into the flour which had been previously
pinned or blocked up at one end of the trough, and mix it well into
the flour with the hands—sprinkle a little flour over the top, and let
it stand five or six hours, during which time the sponge will have
risen twice. The first rising is suffered to break and go down. In
about an hour or so, according to the heat of the bakehouse, the sponge
rises a second time, and just as it is about again to break, or when
the air escapes by the bursting of the bubbles, a sufficient quantity
of water (about three pailsful) to make up the batch is poured into the
sponge from the seasoning tub, the water having dissolved in it pre-

viously about four pounds of salt and eight ounces of what is called stuff—(some use more than a pound or sixteen ounces of stuff). The liquor ought to be well mixed with the sponge; which being done, the pin-board is taken away, and the whole of the flour is well worked up into one mass, which is blocked up by the pin-board to one end, and left about an hour in summer, and two hours in winter, to prove; the vacant part of the trough is then sprinkled with flour to prevent the dough from sticking, the pin-board is knocked out, and the dough is pitched out of the trough on to the lid of the opposite trough, when it is cut into masses and weighed — technically *scaled off.* These masses are then moulded into shape and put aside in a regular manner, to be finally moulded into loaves, taking care to mould those first which were first *scaled off.* Previous to the moulding, the oven must be well *swabbed out,* or cleaned with the swabber or scuttle, and the up-sets chalked to prevent the bread sticking to them. They are then placed at the back and on each side of the oven by means of the peel; the long loaves, or the quartern and half-quartern bricks, are put into the oven, packed together as close as possible—the common round bread is also packed close—but the cottage bread must be placed separately, each loaf by itself, or it will not be crusted all round. After placing the loaves in the oven, or, as the bakers say, *setting the batch,* which requires a good hand to do properly, an up-set is placed in front of it. The potatoes for the next *ferment* are put into a tin or iron kettle, generally round, but sometimes in the form of a fish-kettle, and placed in the oven to boil. When the potatoes are done, and while they are hot, the ferment for the next batch must be mixed. Twenty-four hours elapse from the mixing the ferment to the time when the bread is taken out of the oven.

SUBSTITUTE FOR WHEAT-FLOUR BREAD.

Under this head we intend to treat of the various substitutes which have been used at different times, and in different countries, for bread made of wheat flour. We allude to bread made of rye, barley, oats, peas, beans, buckwheat, maize, farinaceous roots, and of mixed substances, &c. This subject is not without interest, independent of utility, and a work of this kind would scarcely be complete if it were not introduced. We shall enter upon it with few general remarks.

Bread Corn — properly so called, of which bread is made in this country, and other civilized nations, comprehends the seeds of all *cerealia,* or farinaceous grass-like plants, for they all contain a farinaceous or mealy substance of a like nature; and which substance is chiefly composed of starch. The seeds or grain in common use are, first and principally, *wheat;* second, *rye;* and third, *barley.*

Wheat is the only grain from which really good, porous, or light bread can be made; but rye and barley are occasionally used, as well as other grain. The bread, however, is of an inferior quality. A sort of bread is also made from *oats, maize, rice, millet,* &c.

Rice is said, and no doubt truly, to nourish more human beings than all the other seeds together used as food ; and it is by many con sidered the most nutritive of all kinds of grain. Accum, in the *Art of making Bread,* says, that " it has been ascertained, that one part of rice contains as much food and useful nourishment as six of wheat ;" an assertion by the way which we are much inclined to disbelieve. But be this as it may, there is no doubt that rice makes a very nourishing and healthy food, notwithstanding the prejudices that prevailed against it, on the unfounded allegation that it caused diseases in the eye. Rice is the principal food of most of the eastern nations, a fact which shows that it is not unhealthy. Rice is not, however, often made into bread without the addition of flour, and when it is, it forms a loaf of very inferior quality.

Maize is frequently employed as bread-corn in America, but it will not by itself make good loaf-bread ; but unleavened cakes are mad‹ of it, very nutritive and palatable.

Oatmeal is seldom used for making loaf-bread, but is extensively used in the north of Great Britain in making unleavened bread, com monly called oat-cakes. It may be observed here, that the objection to biscuits, oat-cakes, maize-cakes, and other unleavened bread, on the ground of their being unhealthy, and of course not nutritive, appears to be without foundation. There can be no doubt, however, that they are inferior as food to good wheaten loaf-bread.

The seeds of leguminous plants, such as pease and beans, are sometimes used as substitutes for bread-corn. They yield a great deal of meal, which is of a sweetish taste, but it forms a coarse bread, and is generally considered neither palatable nor digestible. Dr. Cullen says, that "on certain farms in his country, upon which the leguminous seeds are produced in great abundance, the labouring servants are much fed upon this kind of grain; but if such servants are removed to a farm upon which the *leguminous seeds* are not in such plenty, and they are, therefore, fed with the *cerealia* (wheat, barley, &c.), they soon find a decay of strength ; and it is common for servants, in making such removals, to insist on their being provided daily, or weekly, with a certain quantity of the leguminous meal." It does not, however, follow, that pease or bean-flower bread would be found generally so nutritive or digestible as wheat-flour bread. A great deal may be attributed to habit, and the laborious employment of farmers' servants in the open air.

All the vegetable substances from which bread is made, contain more or less of *starch,* or what is otherwise called amylaceous fecula, and this is the most valuable and nutritive part of all such substances, whether they consist of grain, or roots, &c.

We scarcely need observe, that the potatoe, amongst roots, is the most extensively used as a substitute for bread. In many countries, particularly Ireland, it is almost the exclusive food of the poor. The potatoe contains a great deal of starch.

Rice, notwithstanding its rough and dry qualities, as a farinaceous vegetable, is capable of being converted into bread, without the addition of any other substance. The Americans, however, make bread of rice by washing it in water till perfectly clean. They then, after the rice has been sufficiently drained, put it into a mortar, and reduce it while damp into a sort of powder; it is then completely dried, and passed through a hair-sieve. The flour thus obtained, it is said, is then generally mixed with a little Indian corn meal, and boiled into a thickish consistence, which is sometimes mixed with boiled potatoes, and fermented and baked in tins, or pans, in the usual manner. The bread, we are told, made in this way, is light and wholesome— " pleasing to the eye, and agreeable to the taste."

But a sort of bread may be made from rice, without the addition of any other kind of meal. Let a sufficient quantity of rice-flour be put into a kneading trough, and at the same time let a due proportion of flour be boiled, into which throw a few handsful of rice in the grain, and boil it till it is broken. This compound will form a thick and viscous substance, which is poured upon the flour, and the whole is kneaded with a mixture of salt and yeast, or other fermenting matter. The dough is then covered with flannel or other cloths to keep it warm, and left to rise. This dough, though firm at first, in the course of fermentation becomes as liquid as soup, and is quite incapable of being worked into loaves, in the usual manner, by the hand. The following is the mode by which this difficulty is surmounted:—The oven is heated while the dough is rising; and it being sufficiently hot, the dough is put into a tin pan, which is covered with a paper, or large leaves. The tin is then placed in the oven, and immediately reversed or turned upside down; the heat prevents the dough from spreading, and, in fact, fixes it in that shape given it by the stewpan or box. This bread is said to be " both beautiful and good;" but when it gets stale, it becomes very much deteriorated — as indeed does all bread in which there is rice.

Potatoes, mixed in various proportions with meal, are frequently employed in the making of bread. The London bakers all use them in greater or less quantities — not, as they say, to save flour, but to assist fermentation. There are various ways in which potatoes may be used with meal in the production of bread, — potatoes alone will not make good bread; the potatoe is not of an adhesive quality, and the bread is not only brown and heavy, but crumbles to pieces. M. Parmentier, to render it more adhesive, mixed with the potatoe-meal a decoction of bran, and sometimes honey and water; either of which, he says, much improved it, by rendering it lighter, better coloured, well tasted, and sufficiently consistent.

He obtained also, he adds, well-fermented bread, of a good colour and taste, by mixing some potatoe pulp with meal of wheat, or potatoe-meal, with the addition of yeast and salt. After repeated trials, he recommends, in times of scarcity, a mixture of potatoes with the meal of wheat, in preference to the meal of any other grain. Where no flour or grain can be obtained, Parmentier recommends the use of bread made from the amylaceous (partaking of starch) powder of potatoes, — potatoe pulp, mixed and fermented, with the addition of honey. Potatoe-meal, when mixed with water, acquires a gluey consistence, but bread made from this and the flour of wheat is never of a good colour. That, however, which is made of a mixture of the pulp with the flour of wheat, is much whiter. Parmentier, we are informed, made bread very much resembling that of wheat, by mixing four ounces of amylaceous powder of potatoes, one drachm of mucilage, extracted from barley, one drachm of the bran of rye, and one drachm of glutinous matter, dried and pounded into powder.

A German writer upon country affairs, of the name of Khyogg, who has obtained the name of the Rustic Socrates, recommends, that potatoes well boiled and carefully peeled should be put into a kneading-trough, covered with boiling water, and beaten or bruised till they are converted into a kind of soup, throughout of one consistence. This soup may be mixed with the flour of wheat in the proportion of one-fourth, one-third, and even one-half; and if the flour be of good quality, the bread will be found pleasant, nourishing, and wholesome. This is the principal food of the peasantry in German Lorraine, and the people of that country are remarkable for their healthy, robust, and vigorous constitutions; the young men are tall and handsome, and the country is thickly populated.

In Vogstand and in Saxony, potatoes are prepared for bread by peeling them, grating them very fine, and by putting the pulp into a milk-pail, or some other suitable vessel. It is then mixed with cold water, which is allowed to remain upon the pulp twenty-four hours. The water is then drawn off, and other water added, and again drawn till the water comes off quite pure. The potatoe pulp is then drained through a clean cloth, and then spread upon a plate, or some other surface, till dry. After this, it is reduced to a fine powder, mixed with an equal portion of wheat flour, and made into bread by the usual process.

We have thought it right to lay before our readers the various ways in which it has been recommended to employ potatoes in making bread in times of scarcity; but after all, our own opinion is, that the best and most economical mode of using potatoes is simply to boil them as they do in Ireland, where, it is much to be regretted, they stand instead of all other food to the mass of the population.

Many other substances have been employed in making bread other than those of the flour of farinaceous vegetables, such as wheat, barley, rye, Indian-corn, oats, &c. The latter grain makes an excellent unleavened bread, and is much eaten in Scotland, Lancashire, and several of the northern English counties. It is called oat-cake, and is preferred by many persons to wheaten bread.

Bread made of Roots.—M. Parmentier, late chief Apothecary in the Hotel des Invalides, whose authority we have before quoted, has published numerous and very curious experiments on the vegetables, which in times of scarcity might be used in the subsistence of animals, as substitutes for those usually employed for that purpose. The result of these experiments in the mind of M. Parmentier was, that starch is the nutritive part of farinaceous vegetables, and that the farina of plants was identical with the starch of wheat. The plants from which he extracted this farina are the bryony, the iris, gladiolus, ranunculus, fumaria, arum, dracunculus, mandragora, colchicum, filipendula, helleborus, and the roots of the gramen caninum arvense, or dog grass of the fields.

The mode employed by M. Parmentier to extract the starch, or farina, from these vegetables, was merely bruising and boiling. The roots were cleansed and scraped, then reduced to a pulp, which being soaked in a considerable quantity of water, a white sediment is deposited, which when properly washed and dried will be found to be pure starch. M. Parmentier converted this starch into bread by mingling it with an equal quantity of potatoes reduced to a pulp, and employing the usual quantity of yeast or other leaven. The bread, we are informed, had no bad taste, and was of excellent quality.

From these experiments of M. Parmentier, it appears, that it is chiefly the amylaceous matter or starch of grain that is nutritious; and, that the nutritive quality of other vegetable substances depends in a great measure on the quantity of that matter which they contain. Starch formed into a jelly, and diffused in water, will keep a long time without change.

Ragwort.—Bread has been made in times of scarcity from the roots of this plant. When ragwort root is first taken out of the ground, it is soft and viscous, but becomes hard in a short time, and may be preserved in that state for years without being at all deteriorated, providing it be kept in a dry, airy place. When this root is ground and reduced to flour, which it may easily be, it has an agreeable nut-like taste. It is said to be easily digested when made into bread, and to be more nutritive and "exhilarating," than wheaten bread. The same properties and effects are attributed to radishes, but we apprehend not truly.

Turnip Bread—is made of turnips mixed with equal quantities of wheat flour. The turnips must be first washed clean, then pared and boiled. Mash them and press the water out of them — at least the greater part. Mix with an equal quantity in weight of coarse meal flour—make the dough in the usual manner, and when risen, form it into loaves, and bake it rather more than ordinary bread; when taken from the oven it will be light and sweet, with a little taste of the turnip. "After it has been allowed to stand," says our authority, "twelve hours, the taste of the turnips is scarcely perceptible, and the smell is quite gone. After an interval of twenty-four hours, it cannot be known that it has turnips in its composition, although it has still a peculiar sweetish taste: it appears to be rather superior to bread made only of wheat flour, is fresher and moister, and even after a week continues very good." We are of opinion, however, that it cannot be so good as wheat bread; for, independent of other considerations, turnips do not contain so much starch or nutritive matter as wheat.

Apple Bread. — A bread said to be very superior to potatoe bread has been made from the use of common apples with meal. Boil one-third of peeled apples; while quite warm, bruise them into two-thirds of flour, including the proper quantity of leaven, or yeast; knead without water, the juice of the fruit being quite sufficient. When this mixture has acquired the consistency of paste, put it into a vessel to rise for about twelve hours. By this process may be obtained a very sweet bread, full of eyes and extremely light.

Meslin Bread. — A good bread is made in many parts of England from what is called meslin, which is a mixture of rye and wheat. This is raised on one and the same ground at the same time, and passes through the processes of reaping, thrashing, grinding, and dressing, in the mixed state.

Salep Bread.—Dr. Percival recommends the employment of orchis root in powder, or, as it is called, salep. He says, that an ounce of salep, dissolved in a quart of water, and mixed with two pounds of flour, two ounces of yeast, and eighty grains of salt, produced a remarkably good loaf, weighing three pounds two ounces; while a loaf made of an equal quantity of the other ingredients, without the salep, or powdered orchis root, weighed but two pounds twelve ounces. If the salep be in too large quantities, its peculiar taste will be distinguishable in the bread.

Oat and Barley Bread.—The Norwegians, we are informed, make bread of barley and oatmeal baked between two stones. This bread, it is added, improves by age, and may be kept thirty or forty years!! At their great festivals, they use their oldest bread; and it is not unusual, at the baptism of a child, to have bread that was baked at the baptism of the grandfather.

Debretzen Bread. — In some parts of Hungary, Debretzen for instance, they have a peculiar mode of fermenting bread without yeast, by means of a leaven made in the following manner. Two large handsful of hops are boiled in four quarts of water; this decoction is poured upon as much wheaten bran as it will moisten, and to this are added four or five pounds of leaven. When the mass is warm, the ingredients are well worked together, so as to be thoroughly mixed. It is then deposited in a warm place for twenty-four hours, and afterwards divided into small pieces, about the size of hens' eggs, which are dried by being placed upon a board and exposed to dry air, but not to the sun; when dry, they are laid up for use, and may be kept for six months.

The following is given as the mode by which bread is made from the above-described ferment. For baking six large loaves, six good handsful of these balls are dissolved in seven or eight quarts of warm water — this mixture is poured through a sieve at one end of the bread-trough, and after it three quarts of warm water, the remaining mass being well pressed out. The liquor is mixed up with flour sufficient to form one large loaf; they then strew this mass over with flour, the sieve with its contents is put upon it, and the whole is covered up and kept warm and left to rise, or till the flour upon it begins to crack. Fifteen quarts of warm water, in which six handsful of salt have been dissolved, are then poured upon it through the sieve; the necessary quantity of flour is added, and the whole is well kneaded together. The dough is then covered up and kept warm for half an hour. It is then formed into loaves which are kept for another half hour in a warm room; and after that they are put into an oven, where they remain for two or three hours according to their size.

There is certainly an advantage in this kind of ferment—which is, its capability of keeping for a long time, and of being made in large quantities. On this account it would be convenient on board of ships, or in the camp of an army.

Millet Bread.—Bread made of millet, if eaten when warm, is pretty palatable, but when cold, it becomes dry and crumbly. Besides, though nutritive when boiled, it is not so in bread, but becomes a very powerful astringent. According to Pliny, however, it would appear, that millet was in very general use as food in Italy among the peasantry. "There is no grain," he says, "more heavy, or which swells more in baking." Probably the Italians had some method for counteracting its astringent properties. It is said to be an excellent leaven, and has been recommended for malting.

Maize Bread—is made of maize, or Indian-corn flour, which is in common and extensive use in nearly all parts of North and South America. Knead the flour with a little salt and water into a stiff mass — roll out into thin cakes, and bake on a hot iron. A hoe is frequently used in America. Another kind of maize bread is called

Homminy Cake. — To make this the Indian-corn, freed from the husks, is boiled with a small portion of French beans, until the whole becomes a pulp; this is made into cakes, and baked over hot embers, or it may be eaten in the pulp, which is frequently the case.

Bean Flour Bread.—Take a quarter of a peck of bean flour and one ounce of salt; mix it into a thick batter with water—pour a sufficient quantity of this batter to make a cake in an iron kettle; and bake over the fire; it will require frequent turning.

Buckwheat Bread — is thus directed to be made by the Board of Agriculture: Take a gallon of water, set it over a fire, and when it boils, let a peck of buckwheat flour be mixed with it, little by little, and keep the mixture constantly stirred, to prevent any lumps being formed, till a thick batter is made. Then add two or three ounces of salt, set it over the fire again, and allow it to boil an hour and a half; pour the proper proportion for a cake into an iron kettle, and bake it.

Acorn Bread — is made of ripe acorns deprived of their husks or skins, and beaten into a paste. To extract the astringent quality of the acorns, put the paste into water for a night, and then press the water from the paste. The mass when dried and powdered must be kneaded up into a dough with water, and raked out into thin cakes, which may be baked over embers. This bread is said not to be disagreeable, and no doubt was considered a great luxury by our British ancestors in the time of the oak-worshipping Druids.

Oatmeal Cakes are thus made: — To a peck of oatmeal add a few table-spoonsful of salt; knead into a stiff paste with warm water; roll the paste into thin cakes, and bake it in an oven, over a hot iron plate, or on embers. Sometimes oat-cake is fermented a little, which makes the cakes light and porous.

Oatmeal and Pease Bread. — To a peck of pease flour, and a like quantity of oatmeal, previously well mixed, by passing the two flours through a sieve, add three or four ounces of salt; knead into a stiff mass with warm water; roll out into thin cakes; and bake in an oven. In some parts of Lancashire and Scotland, this kind of bread is made into flattened rolls, and they are usually baked in an iron pot.

Chestnut Bread — is made from horse-chestnuts, which are seldom or never used for food in this country, though their nutritious qualities are well known to the people in the southern parts of Europe, particularly in some districts of Italy, and in the island of Corsica, where it is the chief and almost the whole of the food of the peasantry. To make this bread, take a peck of horse-chestnuts; peel the skins off them; let them be bruised into a paste; dilute the mass with water, which destroys their astringency, and then strain them through a sieve; a milky liquor is thus separated, which on standing deposits a fine white powder; this, on being dried and ground into flour, is found to be without smell or flavour. It is then made up, sometimes by itself, and not unfrequently with an equal portion of wheat flour, into a paste, with warm milk and a little salt, and when baked makes a very eatable bread.

Potatoe Bread. — Boil the potatoes, and rub them through a cullen der or sieve, and, while hot, rub them in with the flour, which ought to be previously dried. The potatoes should be in proportion to the flour of one-third or one-half. Milk and water is sometimes used for making potatoe bread.

Rye Bread—Barley Bread— and bread made of equal parts of rye flour and wheat flour, or of equal parts of barley flour, rye flour, and wheat flour—are made in the same way as already described. Milk, or milk and water, is preferred, in making rye bread, to pure water.

The Bread Tree.—Various substances have been employed in different parts of the world as substitutes for making bread, in the absence of farinaceous or flour-yielding vegetables. The bread tree, or rather the fruit of this tree, ranks first among the substances alluded to. The bread tree is common in many parts of the east. It is very abundant at Surinam, where extensive avenues may be seen of it, loaded with luxuriant crops of fruit. As a brief account of this extraordinary tree cannot fail to be interesting to our readers (previous to giving a description of the mode of preparing the fruit for food), we beg to lay before them the following remarks and extracts.

All the species of the bread fruit tree, of which there are eight, are natives of the South Sea islands. More than one hundred and fifty years ago, this tree had excited great interest amongst Europeans, and particularly amongst the people of Great Britain. Dampier, who performed his voyage round the world in 1688, thus describes it:—

"The bread fruit as we call it, grows on a large tree as big and high as our largest apple trees; it hath a spreading head, full of branches and dark leaves. The fruit grows on the boughs like apples; it is as big as a penny loaf when wheat is at five shillings the bushel; it is of a round shape, and hath a thick tough rind. When the fruit is ripe it is yellow and soft, and the taste is sweet and pleasant. The natives of Guam use it for bread. They gather it when it is full grown, while it is green and hard; then they bake it in an oven, which scorcheth the rind and maketh it black; but they scrape off the black crust, and there remains a tender thin crust; and the inside is soft, tender, and white, like the crumb of a penny loaf. There is neither *core* nor *stone* in the inside, but all is of a pure substance like bread. It must be eaten new, for if kept more than twenty-four hours, it becomes hard and choaky; but it is very pleasant before it is too stale. This fruit lasts in season eight months in the year; during which the natives eat no other sort of bread kind. I did never see this fruit anywhere but here. The natives told us there was plenty of this fruit growing on the rest of the Ladrone islands; and I did never hear of it anywhere else."

So much for Dampier's account, which, however, does not appear to be quite correct. The great circumnavigator, Cook, thus describes the fruit in question:—"It grows on a tree about the size of a middling oak. Its leaves are frequently a foot and a half long, of an oblong shape, deeply sinuated like those of the fig-tree, which they resemble in consistence and colour, and in the exuding of a white milky juice upon being broken. The fruit is about the size and shape of a child's head, and the surface is reticulated, not much unlike a truffle. It is covered with a thin skin, and hath a core about as big as the handle of a small knife. The eatable part lies between the skin and the core. It is as white as snow, and somewhat of the consistence of new bread. It must be roasted before it is eaten; being divided into three or four parts. Its taste is insipid, with a slight sourness, somewhat resembling that of the crumb of wheaten bread mixed with a Jerusalem artichoke."

The above is the sober and satisfactory account of the bread tree and its fruit, as given by the illustrious Cook. Dr. Hawkesworth's description of its advantages is amusing, but extravagant. He says, "if a man plants ten bread fruit trees in his lifetime, which he may do in about an hour, he will as completely fulfil his duty to his own and future generations, as the natives of our less temperate climate can by ploughing in the cold winter, and reaping in the summer's heat, as often as those seasons return. Even if, after he has procured bread for his present household, he should convert the surplus into money, and lay it up for his children."

The bread fruit tree has been planted in some of the West India colonies, but with little success as to any advantages to be derived from it. Indeed, its fruit appears to us to have been greatly exaggerated with respect to its beneficial application as food for the use of man. It has been observed, however, that "even in those colonies into which the bread fruit has not been generally introduced as an article of food, it is used as a delicacy; or whether employed as bread, or in the form of pudding, it is considered as highly palatable by the European inhabitants."

Bread Fruit Bread.—To prepare the fruit for use instead of bread, it must be roasted, either whole, or cut into three or four pieces. It is also cooked in an oven, which renders it soft, and something like a boiled potatoe; not quite so mealy as a good one, but more so than those of an inferior description. The Otaheitans make three dishes of it, by putting either milk or the milk of cocoa-nut to it, then beating it to a paste with a stone pestle, and afterwards mixing it with ripe plantains, bananas, or mahie.

This mahie is a preparation of the ripe bread fruit, for which it is substituted during the season, just before gathering a fresh crop. It is made thus:—The fruit is gathered just before it is perfectly ripe, and being laid in heaps, is closely covered with leaves; in this state it undergoes a fermentation, and becomes disagreeably sweet. The core is then taken out entire, by gently pulling the stalk, and the fruit is thrown into a hole which is dug for that purpose, generally in the houses, and neatly lined in the bottom and sides with grass; the whole is then covered with leaves, and heavy stones laid upon them. In this state it undergoes a second fermentation, and becomes sour; after which it undergoes no change for many months. It is taken out of the hole as it is wanted for use, and being made into balls, it is wrapped up in leaves, and roasted or baked. After it is baked, it will keep five or six weeks. It is eaten both cold and hot, and the natives seldom make a meal without it. To Europeans, however, the taste is said to be as disagreeable as that of a pickled olive generally is the first time it is eaten.

Sago Bread—is made from the wood of the sago tree, in the follow ing manner:—The natives of the islands of Banda and Amboyna saw the body of the tree into small pieces, and, after bruising and beating them in a mortar, pour water upon the fragments. This is left for some hours undisturbed, to let the pithy farinaceous matter subside. The water is then poured off, and the meal, being properly dried, is formed into cakes, or fermented and made into bread, which, it is said, is nearly as palatable as wheaten bread. The Hottentots make a kind of bread from another species of sago tree. The pith of this tree is collected, and tied up in dressed calf, or sheep-skin, and then buried in the ground for several weeks, which renders .t mellow and tender. It is then made into cakes, which are baked under hot embers. Others roast the sago tree pith, and make it into a kind of porridge.

The sago of commerce is made from the pith of this tree, but it is granulated by passing it through a sieve. It acquires its brown colour from drying it on hot stones.

Casava Bread — is made in the Caribbee Islands, from a very poisonous root called *Jatropa Maniat*, rendered wholesome by the extraction of its acrid juice, which the Indians use for poisoning their arrows. So powerfully poisonous is this juice, that a tea-spoonful is sufficient to take away the life of a man. The root of the *maniat*, after being washed, scraped clean, and grated in a tub, is enclosed in a sack made of rushes, of very loose texture. This sack is suspended upon a stick placed upon two wooden forks. A heavy vessel is suspended to the bottom of the sack, and is so contrived as to press the juice out of the roots. When the juice is all taken from the roots, they become a sort of starch, which is exposed to smoke in order to dry it; when well dried, it is passed through a sieve: it is now called casava. It is baked into cakes by laying it on hot plates of iron, or on hot earth. The article called *tapioca* is the finest part of casava, collected and formed into small tears, by straining the mass, while it is still moist, so as to make it into small irregular lumps.

Plantain Bread—is made from the fruit of the plantain tree. This fruit is about a foot long, and from an inch and a half to two inches in diameter, and has a tough skin, within which there is a soft pulp, of a sweet flavour. The fruit is generally cut when green; the skin is taken off, and the heart is roasted in a clear cold fire for a few minutes: it is then scraped, and served up as bread. This tree is a native of the East Indies, and other parts of the Asiatic continent, but is cultivated on an extensive scale in Jamaica. It is said, that without this fruit the West India islands would be scarcely inhabitable, as no species of provisions could supply its place. Wheaten bread flour is not so agreeable to the negroes, and they greatly prefer it to the fruit of the bread tree.

Banana Bread—is made of the fruit of the banana tree. This fruit is about four or five inches long, of the shape of a cucumber, and of a high ` · grateful flavour. They grow in bunches that weigh twelve pounds and upwards. The pulp of the banana tree is softer than that of the plantain tree, and of a more luscious taste. When ripe it is a very pleasant food, either undressed, or fried in slices like fritters. All classes of people in the West Indies are very fond of it. When preparing for a voyage, they take the ripe fruit and squeeze it through a sieve; then form the mass into loaves, which are dried in the sun, or baked on hot ashes, having been previously wrapped up in leaves.

Moss Bread, or bread made of moss, is prepared from a species of the tribe *lichen,* called rein-deer moss, which contains a considerable quantity of starch. The Icelanders form the *lichen islandicus* into bread, and it is said to be very nutritive. The moss is collected in the summer, dried, and ground into powder — of which bread gruel and pottage are made. It is also boiled in milk or whey, till it comes to a jelly. It should be previously steeped some hours in warm water, in order to extract the bitter matter with which it is impregnated, which is not only disagreeable as to taste, but is also a purgative.

Dried Fish Bread.—We have shown that a great variety of substances are used as substitutes for flour bread. We now come to dried fish. which appears to be an odd thing to make bread of. In Iceland, Lapland, Crim Tartary, and other parts of the north, a kind of bread is made of dried fish, beaten first into powder, sometimes with the inner bark of trees, and then made up into cakes.

Earth Bread.—But the strangest substitute for corn bread that has ever been employed, is a kind of white earth found in Upper Lusatia, of which the poor in times of scarcity have frequently made bread. This bread earth, if we may so designate it, is dug out of a hill where salt-petre had formerly been worked. When heated by the sun it cracks, and small globules proceed from it like meal, which ferment when mixed with flour. It is said on good authority, that on this earth, made into bread, many persons have subsisted for a considerable time. An earth very similar is found in Catalonia.

THE END.

Reprint Publishing

FOR PEOPLE WHO GO FOR ORIGINALS.

This book is a facsimile reprint of the original edition. The term refers to the facsimile with an original in size and design exactly matching simulation as photographic or scanned reproduction.

Facsimile editions offer us the chance to join in the library of historical, cultural and scientific history of mankind, and to rediscover.

The books of the facsimile edition may have marks, notations and other marginalia and pages with errors contained in the original volume. These traces of the past refers to the historical journey that has covered the book.

ISBN 978-3-95940-101-2

Made in
Germany

www.reprintpublishing.com